To Thone

Wee White Blossom

What Post-Referendum Scotland Needs To Flourish

Thanks for the great atmosphere you created!

LESLEY RIDDOCH

Luath Press Limited

EDINBURGH

www.luath.co.uk

First published 2015

ISBN: 978-1-908373-99-1

The paper used in this book is recyclable. It is made from
low chlorine pulps produced in a low energy, low emissions
manner from renewable forests.

Printed and bound by
Martins the Printers, Berwick upon Tweed

Typeset in 10.5 point Sabon

To Rosie and Jenny,
joyful young companions
on the journey

Contents

Acknowledgements   9

Introduction   11

CHAPTER ONE   2014: Scotland's Year of Living
                   Dangerously   19

CHAPTER TWO   Radical Scotland meets the Smith
                   Commission   35

CHAPTER THREE   Blossom   46

CHAPTER FOUR   Land, Land Everywhere... and
                   Soon a Drop for Sale   58

CHAPTER FIVE   Supersized Councils –
                   Disempowered Communities   70

CHAPTER SIX   Women – The Real Indyref
                   Winners   82

CHAPTER SEVEN   What's Next – The 2015 General
                   Election   103

CONCLUSION   What Scotland Needs to Blossom   113

Acknowledgements

Muriel Alcorn
Bella Caledonia
Øivind Bratberg
Paddy Bort
Robin Callander
Hannah Derbyshire
Development Trusts Association Scotland
Professor Tom Devine
Foster Evans
Maggie Fyffe
Jim Harvey
Mary Hepburn
Luath Press, Kirsten Graham and Louise Hutcheson
Cathy McCormack
Professor David McCrone
Professor Catriona MacDonald
Rosemarie MacEachen
Cailean MacLean
Robin McAlpine
Annie Macsween
Professor Charles McKean
Mark Perryman
Perspectives magazine, especially Davie Laing
Tommy Riley
Mona Røhne
The Scotsman

The Sunday Herald
Newsnet Scotland
The National
Tore Tanum
Ann Soutar
Phil Welsh
Andy Wightman
Raymond Young

All the above have saved me from errors in fields where they are expert and the faults or misjudgements that survive their amendments are mine alone.

Introduction

Wee White Blossom is a post-referendum update for folk who have already read the main book. Parts of the original are included to give context and make this diminutive version readable. Doubtless by the time you read this, though, some thoughts will be out-dated, slightly off-beam or even plain wrong. Events in Scotland after the referendum are moving that fast. Unfortunately some of the main *Blossom* chapters, like the one about Tommy Riley and the Drumchapel Men's Health project, cannot now change. Tommy died prematurely of COPD just before *Blossom* was first published in 2013. Consultant obstetrician Mary Hepburn has now (partly) retired to her beloved Shetland. The lives of the drug-using mothers she treated in Possil and North Glasgow are still grim. The bold housing pioneers of West Whitlawburn have gone from strength to strength despite the sad death of co-founder Phil Welsh. They are currently installing a district heating system to save energy and cut bills – meanwhile much of council-run East Whitlawburn looks set to be demolished.

But of course there has been even bigger change in Scotland since 2013. 45 per cent of Scots voted Yes in the independence referendum – more than anyone could dream of when this book was first published but not enough to win the day. Since that vote, with its record-breaking 85 per cent turnout, pro-independence movements like Women for Independence,

Radical Independence, National Collective and Common Weal have flourished and party membership has surged amongst Yes supporting parties like the Greens, ssp and above all the snp – likely to have 100,000 members by Burns Night 2015. Nicola Sturgeon was elected unopposed as the new snp leader and has already made history three times – she is the first female snp leader, the first female First Minister and leads the first gender equal cabinet. Not bad going for one week. The Scottish Government's new legislative programme contains a long overdue Land Reform Bill, plans for more affordable childcare and quotas for women on public boards. Meanwhile Alex Salmond has announced he will contest the 2015 Westminster elections as a candidate for the Gordon constituency, breathing yet more life into the hyper-oxygenated snp.

Of course there is some anxiety about keeping new members engaged, a dearth of independent candidates willing to stand 'under the snp banner' and disappointment amongst time-served members about the number of recently-joined folk competing for 2015 nominations. But in the former Yes camp, the air is full of possibility.

By contrast, the main victors of the No campaign, the Labour Party, have been tearing themselves apart – or retiring. Johann Lamont resigned unexpectedly in the wake of the No vote. She described Westminster Labour mps as dinosaurs and accused the London leadership of treating the Scottish party like a branch office. Alistair Darling and Gordon Brown led the No camp to victory – then each (separately) announced his intention to leave politics in 2015, giving the appearance that No leaders had cut and run before 'substantial new powers' were wrestled from Westminster – whilst the blood-ied but unbowed Salmond was preparing to soldier on.

Of course hardcore Labour supporters will not see the Brown/ Darling retirement announcements that way at all. But a perception of constancy could help the SNP win the all-important battle over the narrative of the 2015 campaign. General Elections have hitherto been perceived by Scots as a two-horse race in which England votes (largely) Tory so Scotland must vote (largely) Labour. But the next election looks set to produce another hung parliament in which neither party alone has a working majority. That opens up the prospect of a different dynamic – a four-horse race as UKIP take seats south of the border while the SNP is elected in large numbers north of it. In this scenario, an SNP vote doesn't contribute to a Tory victory (Nicola Sturgeon has said she will 'never, ever support a Conservative government') but could make a Labour government with SNP backing more likely. Of course a sizeable SNP bloc will try to extract full Home Rule for Scotland and the cancellation of Trident's renewal – and that might be a political price too high for Ed Miliband without losing even more support in Middle England. Still, such a scenario might serve to reinforce the SNP's role as guarantor of Scottish interests at Westminster. As Salmond said on the BBC's *Sunday Politics*, 'The only circumstances in which people will trust Labour to deliver for Scotland is when the SNP are at their heels.'

With five months to go, that rhetoric may resonate strongly with disgruntled Scottish voters.

Far more certain though, is that Salmond already resonates

with the UK media. Having spent the election campaign virtually ignoring his very able deputy Nicola Sturgeon, the British
press has built Salmond into a powerful UK phenomenon
which culminated in a Liverpool *Question Time* programme
where the audience applauded Salmond's suggestion they
could 'come with Scotland next time' and laughed as
presenter David Dimbleby was left guessing about Salmond's
intentions for 2015. The former First Minister also bagged
the 2014 Spectator's Politician of the Year award, suggesting
absence from the miserable London scene has only made
right-wing hearts grow fonder of a man who boldly disrupted
Nigel Lawson's budget in 1988 and has gone on to disrupt
British life.

But Salmond's candidacy could have a more important
and immediate impact, ending any chance that General Election TV debates can reasonably exclude the SNP, Greens and
Plaid Cymru. Of course, Salmond is no longer SNP leader and
the controversial decision to exclude 'small' parties except
UKIP 'fits broadcast guidelines'. But it's hard to see how the
BBC can support a deal that places performance above fair-
ness when Mr Box Office himself is in town using every available opportunity to raise the scandal of the SNP's exclusion,
when its party membership would exceed a million in UK terms.
A state broadcaster already facing accusations of referendum
bias could find its credibility seriously damaged by a constant,
Salmond-led chorus of 'we wuz muzzled'.

That's also because Salmond has enjoyed renewed status
since his dignified exit the day after referendum defeat. Many
agree that nothing became him like the manner of his going.

My hairdresser – a traditional Labour voter – was moved to tears by his resignation speech and Salmond's emotional farewell at the SNP conference was followed by an equally affectionate BBC Scotland tribute programme. Perhaps like Sherlock Holmes – whose reincarnation after a highly acclaimed TV 'death' was watched by millions – Alex Salmond is a colourful character the public just don't want to lose.

And yet there are dangers.

Angus Robertson will remain the SNP's official Westminster leader. How easy will that be if the media is constantly seeking out opinions from his erstwhile leader? It could be a canny move if Salmond is allowed to roam the TV and radio studios as Charles Kennedy has done for decades, while someone else makes sure Commons business gets done.

But if the SNP wins 30 or 40 Scottish seats, as polls currently predict, and formally supports Labour, new MPs will be expected to break the habit of 30 years and vote on English matters. That could rankle with some. On the other hand, if an enlarged SNP contingent has no new role in government, party discipline could become an even bigger issue. Some 'non-traditional' candidates are bound to be selected and sent south. And whilst no independent candidate has publicly accepted the offer to stand 'under the SNP banner' (a contradiction in terms for many thrawn, non-party oriented folk like myself), 'newbies' are bound to get restless sitting on the sidelines if they feel Scotland's fate is being determined elsewhere.

Will Alex Salmond's candidacy be a gamechanger for the SNP in 2015 or will the pendulum swing back towards Labour once they have a new Scottish leader?

One thing's certain, though – David Cameron certainly infuriated erstwhile Better Together partners by constantly linking greater powers for Scotland with English votes for English laws.[1] UKIP has won two recent by-elections and England looks set to vote for an EU exit in the forthcoming referendum, pulling a reluctant Scotland along with her. All of this seems to have refocused Scots' minds. One opinion poll just after the vote, suggested a majority of Scots would now vote Yes if the referendum was re-run. It's fair to discount some of that enthusiasm since the proposition is currently theoretical – but such polls leave Scots uncertain that the balance of opinion still wholeheartedly backs the Union. Meanwhile, two other polls – one straight after 18 September and another two months later – found a consistent two-thirds of Scots backing Home Rule, where Holyrood controls all taxation, spending and welfare and sends payment south to Westminster for defence and foreign affairs. Clearly, that 66 per cent contains many folk who voted No to

---

1 The Vow was published on the front page of the *Daily Record* days before the referendum vote and apparently signed by Messrs Cameron, Miliband and Clegg. The three unionist party leaders vowed to agree 'substantial new powers' for the Scottish Parliament before the 2015 general election and delivery by whichever party formed a government. English Votes for English Laws (EVEL) is an attempt to stop MPs with devolved control over taxation from voting on such English matters in the Commons. In fact the SNP has not done that for 30 years. But such a convention or new law would remove the once sizeable contingent of Scottish MPs from the Labour party total – impeding the chances of a future Labour government achieving a working majority for its budget and for new English legislation.

independence. So will this larger and more 'settled will' wrestle Home Rule out of Westminster? Not easily. And certainly not without another massive and co-ordinated demonstration of political will at the 2015 general election. Given the heady levels of activism over the past two years, that is entirely possible.

CHAPTER ONE

2014 – Scotland's Year of Living Dangerously

THE INDEPENDENCE campaign began in earnest for me in September 2013. That month *Blossom* was first published, I began a book and speaking tour that eventually took in 190 venues and started a course of chemotherapy for an auto immune condition called vasculitis. Mercifully I had a fairly mild version of it, with tiny blood vessels going wrong only in my kidneys – it can occur in other organs.

The bad news is that it still can. The good news is that it seems to be contained. So when I said on Question Time that 2014 was the best year of my life, I really meant it. Despite weekly blood tests, three-hour chemotherapy sessions every fortnight until February 2014 and joint problems that left me hurpling for months, 2014 was a topper.

I say this not for sympathy (though if you're thinking of flowers, my favourites are still lupins). Many folk struggle with illness, and I am much better.

I say this because Scotland, lit up by the possibility of real, profound political change, helped me through. The generosity, humour and courage of folk on the referendum trail was quietly inspirational and the luminous beauty of the landscape was breathtaking – in every season.

It was a strange bit of synchronicity. In 2013, I published a book arguing Scots had the capacity to heal their country and themselves. In 2014, I was experiencing the truth of that dynamic myself, at first hand.

Very few people realised anything was wrong – early kidney problems have no symptoms apart from tiredness – so I know what I witnessed was the real deal. In 2014, while animosity reigned in the public arena, kindness was the currency in the local, grassroots and private domains where the Yes campaign flourished.

Folk in far flung places slept on sofas so I got the spare bed. I stayed in the snug Stromness home of a fisherman's mum while she was 'aff sooth.' I shared fresh Hebridean salmon at the home of a retired Free Church Minister in Stornoway, a riotously funny evening with kirk elders in Aberdeen, an eye-opening weekend with the troubled tenant farmers of Islay and a long simmer dim day with musicians on Shetland.

Two young snowboarders from Aviemore took the day off work to organise a mini bike tour – and wait for me without complaint at the top of every hill. I sat in some spectacular locations to write newspaper columns fed with home-made and often home-grown food. After one event in Stewarton, I was presented with two blocks of delicious local cheese and a bottle of 'The Optimist' wine. Folk in the poorest communities were always the ones who had a thoughtful whip round to reimburse train fares or petrol costs and non-professional groups seemed to demonstrate the strongest ability to get organised and self-start.

It was *Blossom* in action. Heartening, gratifying and life-affirming. The enthusiasm and frenzied activity was as infectious and self-reinforcing as the previous long decades of forelock-tugging disempowerment. Unexpectedly, and as the by-product of an independence campaign backed by only a minority of voters, the whole of Scotland seemed to be switched on.

One cold Lochinver evening, 40 crofters packed into a tiny side room of the village hall, sitting on each other's laps and standing in door-wells for a *Blossom* talk. Discovering there was only one light switch, which meant pitch-darkness or dazzling light, they rummaged through the cupboards and found tea-lights and a head torch. The meeting went ahead in subdued but flickering light until an older lady at the front, picked up the head torch, squashed it over her newly permed hair and looked up from her seat. 'I'm your spotlight, lass.' A young mum called Raghnaid travelled from Farr to a *Blossom* event in Aberdeen. Back home the next day she chatted enthusiastically to another mum at the local play park. Neither woman had organised a political talk before, but standing at the swings, Raghnaid and Kirsty decided to give it a go. The mums enlisted friends to design, print, laminate and hammer hundreds of posters onto fences beside road junctions within a 20 mile radius of the village. Volunteers replaced the signs up to four times to cope with rain and naysayers. On the night, they produced a PA system, badges, stickers, homemade food and drink, with a donations box to cover expenses and a fabulous, local all-women band to open the gig. Around 250 people finally packed into Farr's tiny remote hall, the discussion lasted for hours and that night Maree – another young mum – went home to Strathpeffer, with the germ of an idea. She spoke to friends about Farr and together they reproduced the same warm and relaxed atmosphere with another capacity audience a few months later.

Since then Maree herself has gone from strength to strength. 'I am much more confident and can-do. I applied for and got one of the few places on a prescribing course and am aiming to combine outpatient clinic appointments with a teaching role – quite cutting edge for pharmacy. So the catalysing effect has definitely gone beyond politics.' This phenomenon – of personal empowerment through political activity – is hugely significant for Scotland. All too often the flow of energy has been the other way around – with individuals feeling disappointed or crushed by their brush with the political world.

In his book *The Tipping Point*, Malcolm Gladwell described 'doers' like Raghnaid, Kirsty and Maree as Mavens; 'almost pathologically helpful… information brokers, sharing and trading what they know' and starting 'word-of-mouth epidemics' due to their knowledge, social skills and ability to communicate.

In Scotland there have always been Mavens in abundance. In 2014, though, they came into their own.

Wings Over Scotland – aka the Rev. Stuart Campbell – grew a substantial readership during the referendum campaign, and raised more than £200,000 from readers to commission polls and produce the 'Wee Blue Book.' Stephen Paton's breathless YouTube alternative news bulletins were a regular fix for many, likewise Greg Moodie's darkly satirical cartoons and Stewart Bremner's languidly lovely designs. Kate Higgins' Burdz Eye View and other blogs abounded. Newsnet Scotland's news coverage and Bella Caledonia's opinion columns came into their own and the irrepressible Zara Gladman clocked up 130 thousand views for her cover of a Lady Gaga song 'Bad Romance' (honest – only 30 thousand of those can really be attributed to me.) And where is the BBC TV series that should be the automatic reward for such a talented bunch of individuals?[1] Predictably, Auntie's awkwardness with independence remains.)

Strangely though, it was the modest communications spoken in private that stayed with me longest.

On Orkney, a single mum came up to speak after the opening of the Yes Shop in Kirkwall's bustling Street. She said she'd just quit her zero hours contract job to work flat out for a Yes vote in the final fortnight. 'With benefit cuts and all the suspicion, I can't cope with Westminster any more. I have to do this.' After a *Blossom* event in Fife, an old man came up to volunteer for action. 'If someone can push the wheelchair I can sit with the leaflets on my lap.' In 2014 inspiration was all around. And of course, travelling from meeting to meeting there was always Scotland herself. I walked through salty foam after a storm on the beach at Storr, collected brambles along the cycle path at Deeside, basked on Berneray during a heatwave and stood by the ancient graves at Finlaggan. I saw grouse flying beside train windows, counted hundreds of deer in Assynt and marvelled at the snow-capped otherworldliness of the Trotternish Ridge on Skye. It was like being in a dream. Indeed, in the hard-bitten months and years ahead, some folk may wonder if all of this actually happened. It did.

Quietly, below the radar, and initially beyond the interest of the mainstream media, momentum gathered. Artists who once described themselves as 'apolitical' joined National Collective's Yestival tour, young folk who'd never voted before turned up at weekends to canvass 'hard to reach' housing

---

[1] At least Greg Moodie now does a regular cartoon for *The National*.

estates and women who'd never discussed politics organised informal, drop-in meetings near schools and shopping centres.

Bit by bit even the most hardened cynics conceded something special was happening. *The Spectator*'s Alex Massie wrote; 'This vigorous political carnival... has been a revolt against politics as usual: a cry, from the heart as much as from the head, for a different way of doing things.'

But actually, grassroots campaigners weren't crying for change – they were creating it. Without seeking permission, waiting for guidance or looking for approval.

And like most transformational change, it was very personal.

My husband – who cancelled work to drive me round during the worst months – began to share my experience, meet the folk I met and reassess his original doubts about independence. Soon he become a multiple badge-wearing enthusiast. One day I came home to discover the word YES in sky-blue paint on the concrete driveway outside our house. 'I dropped a paint can and then thought, why not?' he explained sheepishly. It takes a lot for a man to admit he's wrong. And in any case, he wasn't. He just hadn't previously been engaged. Inside that intoxicating 'can do' environment, his perspective changed because people changed, hesitant, uncertain behaviour changed and Scotland's possibilities as an independent country started to change as well.

Me too. At the start I used to avoid official Yes events fearing immersion in an uncomfortable and unquestioning sort of Yes evangelism.

I was reluctant to wear a Yes badge, preferring to use the guid Scots word Aye. I changed.

We all changed – at least those who made that difficult journey.

And that is what still divides Scots today.

The nature of the path we have recently travelled.

Some folk got up on 18 September and voted No. Some swithered. Others wrestled with the arguments. But most folk on the Yes side did so much more. They got engaged with new people and issues, educated themselves, canvassed others, attended political meetings, wore badges – even at work – found new media sources, spoke in public, booked halls, fund-raised, backed crowd-sourced projects and joined grassroots movements and political parties.

Independence was a difficult destination, supported until that last extraordinary week by fewer than 40 per cent of Scots. And yet in its difficulty lay its beauty. An easy journey demands little of its travellers.

Perhaps that's why the Labour Party is currently in disarray. A difficult journey demands organisation, camaraderie and creative solutions and produces precious things like willpower, stamina and friendship. That's why the independence campaign is merely suspended in the minds of most Yes voters – because the desire for change is not.

Of course it wasn't just a difficult journey. It was a difficult result.

After months of complacency, the No campaign was shocked into action by a final YouGov poll showing 51 per cent support for Yes. A mass rush to Euston followed as 90 Labour MPs headed up to press the flesh and love bomb Glasgow voters – accompanied by a gallus Glaswegian on a rickshaw playing the Imperial Death March from Star Wars, and shouting 'People of Glasgow, welcome your imperial masters.' Only in Glasgow. *The Daily Record* published 'The

Vow' – a mocked-up letter supposedly signed by the three unionist party leaders which committed them to devolving 'substantial new powers' to Holyrood in the event of a No vote. Perhaps though, the most concerted campaign of big business scaremongering in recent British history had a greater impact on voters than the offers dangled in the Vow. ASDA warned food prices could rise if Scots voted Yes – though Morrisons suggested prices might fall, Tesco anticipated no change and the BBC's Economic Editor Robert Peston revealed Number Ten had orchestrated the food price scare in a Downing Street meeting with supermarket chiefs. Naughty. Naughty.

But the press didn't probe that – nor did they ask how ASDA would avoid a Scottish wipe-out if they failed to keep prices low or indeed why prices should rise in the first place. Currently, food produced in Scotland heads down to distribution centres in England before travelling back at great expense. So if independence eliminated these costly and wasteful food miles, food might be cheaper and fresher and the environment might benefit as well.

But most of the Union-supporting press and the BBC simply overlooked all nuance in pursuit of 'the story.'

Standard Life was next to breathe life into the McArmageddon narrative, repeating an earlier threat to move some jobs south in the event of a Yes vote. A day later they watched millions wiped from their share price. The papers blamed the prospects of independence. But markets were clearly also worried about the UK Government's refusal to contingency plan for independence.

Once again, beyond the bare headline, lay some important details. Standard Life didn't threaten a move to London lock, stock and barrel. They suggested some assets and staff might shift – and those in the know thought most staff would stay. Likewise with Lloyds and RBS.

In the end though, business scaremongering and Better Together's vague promise of change proved decisive. Of course, some Scots simply wanted to remain part of the UK. What proportion of voters fell into each category – we'll never know. Overall, the ballot reflected the Scots' worst fears not our highest hopes. That's democracy. 55 per cent of Scots voted No – but the very next day they were rewarded by being put to the back of the constitutional queue while Ed Miliband and David Cameron played political games over English votes for English Laws. The night ended with the sickening spectacle of a Union flag-waving mob terrorising folk in Glasgow's George Square and foggy, heavy air hanging over Holyrood as the Media Village was dismantled. News of Alex Salmond's resignation served as a temporary distraction from the prevailing gloom. All seemed extremely bleak.

So what changed?

Well, over the confused days that followed, a realisation dawned.

No had the votes and a victory on paper. But Yes had momentum and a movement. The vote is over but the movement endures.

One year of living dangerously – daring to trust, organise, connect and cooperate – has proved habit-forming for Scots who once hid behind a protective mask of cynical detachment. Now it's cool to turn up, cool to try – heavens it's even cool to vote and join political parties.

Lordy, lordy. How did that happen?

There was no organisation linking the groups that transformed Yes from a narrow party-led campaign. Nor, to an extent, did there need to be. In contrast to the more hierarchical SNP, the Yes movement let go of the reins from the start – artists congregated around National Collective, activists settled in RIC, women joined Women for Independence, policy wonks headed for Common Weal, and journalists wrote for Newsnet Scotland, Bella Caledonia and others. In the best Scottish tradition there was no single person trying to corral free spirits into one name, campaign, venue or outlook – and indeed people are still happily moving between some or all of these campaigning groups today. The result for many Scots has been a giddy level of engagement, the acquisition of valuable 'soft skills' and membership of a vast community which still shares an unforgettable, intense and shared experience.

My memory of the last few Indyref months contains a hundred images. The sassy video of Lady Alba playing over and over in the Aye Shop on Easter Road in Edinburgh. The woman who turned up asking simply for a hug. The actor Brian Cox who helped settle me before the first TV interview in the Media village outside Holyrood after the No vote. He looked me square in the face and said, in that famous gravelly voice, 'Lesley, remember, the issues have not been resolved. Now go to it. And if you get wobbly, I'll still be standing here.'

Stranger highlights include chumming the outspoken Yes-supporting designer Vivienne Westwood on a frenetic eve of poll Channel Four debate; discreetly slipping my Aye badge to an Asian shopworker in a Tesco store so cameras wouldn't pick up the gesture; receiving my purse in a special delivery bag from a Yes supporter who found it near a petrol station in Inverness (I had set it on the roof and driven off); and sharing a makeshift TV sofa with Pat Kane, Iain Macwhirter, Stephen Paton and Sarah Beattie Smith on the temporary online channel, Referendum TV.

The camaraderie and good will didn't take the Yes vote over the line on 18 September but it did leave a sweeter taste in voters' mouths than the relentlessly negative No campaign. A post-referendum YouGov poll found 60 per cent thought Yes was more positive than negative whilst the same proportion thought No was more negative than positive.

It ain't what you do, it's the way that you do it – and that positive association with the Yes campaign is still shaping public outlooks on a whole range of apparently unrelated issues.

Firstly, many old sources of unimpeachable authority are badly holed below the water line. The BBC in particular had a bad referendum with weekly protests outside its Glasgow HQ and a continuing campaign to withhold licence-fees. Shell, ASDA and Standard Life may have escaped Jim Sillar's 'Day of Reckoning,' but crowd-sourced campaigns to work around these firms through community banks, local energy companies and food cooperatives are thriving. I doubt that's a coincidence. The political clout wielded by status-quo supporting big business has alarmed almost everyone. All voters now understand that with another whiff of serious change, they'll probably be off – or threatening departure to derail democracy again. Do Scots want an economy that relies on companies like these?

Secondly, democratic participation is now at an all-time high. 97 per cent of voters or almost 4.3 million people registered to vote and 85 per cent finally turned out. Despite a shameful attempt to chase newly registered voters for unpaid poll tax debts – skilfully exposed by Alex Salmond in a radio confrontation – we now have a massive, questioning and active electorate – certain to include 16 and 17 year olds as voters once election administration is devolved to Scotland from an implacable and unimpressed Westminster.

Land reform is on the cards thanks to the Land Reform Review Group.

Community control is on the agenda thanks to an impressive change in direction by COSLA and the tireless work of Development Trusts.

Women are now powerful players in Scottish society – thanks in part to Nicola Sturgeon whose calm, surgical dissection of former Scottish Secretary Michael Moore led to his replacement by the more bullish Alistair Carmichael, himself demolished by the impressive new SNP leader in a subsequent TV debate. Sturgeon's approval ratings topped all male contenders including Alex Salmond – in a less sexist society, she would unquestionably have been named 'Person of the Match.' Just as influential, though, was the final narrowing of the once whopping independence gender gap and the altered behaviour of Scotsmen during that final campaign year. As the penny dropped that women held the key to a Yes vote, even mouthy men learned to stand back, bite their tongues and allow women to take the floor. Yes meetings were nearly always gender-balanced, prominent speakers included actress Elaine C Smith and new names like trade unionist Cat Boyd, Women for Independence co-founder Jeane Freeman and Business for Scotland Director Michelle Thompson.

Artwork featured female images. Indeed the Spirit of

Independence fast became the iconic image of the Yes campaign – designed by Stewart Bremner and driven round Scotland on the side of a Blue Goddess fire engine by Dundee's genial giant, the pony-tailed Chris Law.

As each poll revealed a new weak point in the Yes demographic, campaigners put the interests of those social groups before their own.

Empathy flourished. Older gents who might once have been Tartan Tories learned to admire the dogged young street canvassers; tub-thumping 'heart' nationalists acknowledged the persuasive power of speakers like Green co-convenor Patrick Harvie – all seemed stunned when Alex Salmond resigned.

So stands Scotland where it did? Not on your nelly.

The professional classes in Scotland may be busy with Commissions, vows, deals, submissions and General Election preparations but the wider Yes Movement is busy with huge spontaneous meetings involving hundreds, even thousands of people.

Stewart Bremner's Spirit of Independence – the iconic face of the Yes campaign

Forgive a momentary flight of purple prose – but 'meeting' is too small a word. These gatherings are like birds flocking before winter or starlings swooping to throw shapes into darkening skies – because they can. These massive events carry echoes of epic gatherings from our past – when Highland Land Leaguers met in Sutherland glens to demand land reform, women rallied in George Square to launch rent strikes, ship-workers occupied Upper Clyde Shipbuilders and many of my generation marched against the War in Iraq.

They are evangelical, emotional, educational, exciting and slightly exhausting. Like going to a church with purpose, friends but without religion. At least not a conventional religion. They are a way to recharge batteries and suspend the old, hopeless, isolated, directionless way many folks used to lead their political lives.

And no-one wants these days to end – so folk are searching restlessly for the new campaign.

Obviously, it will soon be the 2015 General Election. But meantime women in the Highlands and Common Weal branches are tackling austerity by persuading supermarkets to hand over out-of-date food for local distribution. Green groups have set up fuel banks, so spare wood and coal can be distributed to old people with solid fuel stoves but no cash. Others are setting up Common cafes and energy companies. And every meeting begins with the deposit of bags full of cans, packets and groceries to donate to local food banks. Indeed that is not peculiar to Yes meetings – I spotted a sign asking for donations of heavy winter coats in STV's Dundee studios to hand onto food banks and a journalist friend in Glasgow is trying to organise presents for the oft-forgotten teenage children in families on the breadline. Scots seem to have rediscovered a conscience and a cause – energised by the referendum. Somehow despite losing the war, Yes campaigners are winning the peace.

How unexpected. In centrally run, top down, passive, law-abiding Scotland, people power has finally triumphed. Not amongst all the people – agreed. But amongst enough to have changed the future conduct, priorities, look and sound of political debate.

Like all the best revolutions there was no silver bullet, no single event, no starter's pistol and no paid organisers clutching mission statements and clipboards. Well maybe a few – but mercifully most stayed inside Yes Campaign headquarters. Their early self-absorbed, apparent inactivity was a mistake. But like the error that prompted penicillin's discovery – it was a brilliant, empowering mistake which allowed a movement to grow where once there were only politicians.

At first, local Yes groups expected instructions, resources and directions from HQ. Soon they stopped waiting and started acting. Scots demanding a more equal, grassroots-based and active society became the change they wanted to see.

It was a heady thing to witness.

When Artur Mas visited Scotland in 2013, the Catalan President was envious of Scots – we had a referendum process agreed with London whilst Madrid has refused to even discuss a vote. But by the time he left a week later, the envy had disappeared. Mas observed that the Scottish independence campaign was not a real movement – but a top-down, party-led effort with very little grassroots activism. It was no surprise, he said, that the Scottish vote was stuck around 30 per cent while Catalans had deployed hundreds of thousands of supporters holding hands in a stunning 400-kilometre-long protest from the Pyrenees to the capital Barcelona.

The Catalan leader had a point back then. But not now.

The independence movement grew beyond the vision of one party and surprisingly for schism-prone Scotland, there was remarkably little friction or petty argument. Instead Yes reminded many 50-somethings like myself of the idealistic, hippy days of their youth, infused with artistry and largely devoid of the preciousness that turns so many people off politics. Indeed passive, top-down, over-professionalised, party-controlled politics in Scotland is set for permanent change after 'movement' activists joined the SNP and Greens in their thousands, bringing their permissive, cooperative ideas with them.

Changes at the top mesmerise the media. But simply put, 1.6 million Scots voted Yes to transform Scotland. Such a sizeable number still can.

Within the last few months, previously 'in-active' Scots have been raising cash, setting up new media, creating businesses, hearing new music, seeing new images and graphics, creating choirs and re-establishing vibrancy within their own communities.

That effort hasn't stopped.

These Yes activists can rebuild Scotland from the grassroots if they can focus on issues besides independence, if they can persuade like-minded No voters join them and if a rejuvenated Scottish Government can grasp the nettle and make long-overdue, structural changes to Scottish society.

At long last, the omens are good. Despite the somewhat predictable disappointment of the Smith Commission.

CHAPTER TWO

Radical Scotland meets the Smith Commission

'WHAT IS 'EXTREME' about believing that everyone needs enough food to eat?'

That question was posed by a young Aberdeen delegate at the Radical Independence Conference in late November 2014 and brought a roar from 3,000 activists. Hours later and yards away in the Clyde Arena, Nicola Sturgeon brought 12,000 Yes supporters to their feet speaking of her determination to stop new nuclear weapons being sited on the Clyde.

Meanwhile on the east coast, a relatively tiny Liberal Democrat conference called for welfare powers to be transferred to Holyrood and Labour was rumoured to be ditching its Devo Nano proposals.

Something radical is still in the wintry post referendum Scottish air – due to a number of things. It's an equal and opposite reaction to the UK Government's increasingly right-wing agenda. It's also the product of confidence and consciousness raising during the referendum campaign which has reawakened Scotland's long submerged social democratic instincts.

This positive outlook encouraged Newsquest (the publishers of *The Herald*) to produce Scotland's first ever pro-independence daily newspaper, *The National* two months after the referendum defeat. An experimental week proved so successful that the paper is now a permanent feature – and helps fill a 45 per cent sized hole in the newspaper market which other proprietors unaccountably overlooked. Perhaps the majority Yes vote in Glasgow gave Newsquest the necessary big hint. Yes supporters read newspapers too.

The change in SNP leadership has also prompted a move to the left – so has a growing awareness of how more equal and economically successful Nordic countries operate. But the 'radical' tilt of much Scottish thinking is also due to the under-reported efforts of the New Left – led by Common Weal, National Collective and the Radical Independence Campaign.

This 'loose left' is not explicitly based on the class divisions of previous movements – though it remains acutely aware of their enduring power. Younger folk seem less keen to be labelled or constrained by particular credos. But at the November 2014 RIC conference, all backed the People's Vow – a 'radical' set of goals possibly backed by a majority of the wider Scottish population.

The People's Vow promises to 'multiply the dreaming power of the ordinary Scottish citizen', renationalise industries for the common good, develop more green energy, establish a republic not a monarchy, construct a 'people's budget' as an alternative to austerity, campaign against fracking, push for radical land reform and greater gender equality, work for the rejection of nuclear weapons and Nato and dump the Transatlantic Trade and Investment Partnership, the controversial US-EU trade deal.

For many Scots, that's now a fairly mainstream set of proposals.

RIC speakers included trade unionists, academics, lawyers,

youth campaigners, MSPs, anti-Trident campaigners, writers and journalists as well as Greens, SSP and Common Weal members, feminists and land reform campaigners.

RIC co-founder Jonathan Shafi said: 'We want to be part of the political furniture in Scotland.' With a conference growing from 800 people in 2012 to 3000 in 2014, it already is.

The question is what to do with this movement – generous and inclusive enough to mention the SNP's neighbouring event even though the compliment was not reciprocated.

Actually, it may achieve one objective simply by continuing to exist – it has already nudged mainstream Scots into more radical thinking.

A YouGov poll shows most Scots now think no Westminster leader would make 'the best Prime Minister'. The poll shows each unionist party leader has worse ratings in Scotland than anywhere else in the UK.

Sometimes cautious academics have chosen to stand up and be counted over demands for Scottish Home Rule.

Dr Jim McCormick of the Joseph Rowntree Foundation wanted Scotland to gain powers to tackle poverty. Stirling University's Professor David Bell demanded devolution of the minimum wage and the Scottish Council for Voluntary Organisations called for more tax-raising powers than just the devolution of income tax.

Professor Iain McLean of Oxford University, said devolving the whole of North Sea tax was 'perfectly feasible as well as desirable' – the Chartered Institute of Taxation, the Institute of Chartered Accountants and the Principal of Glasgow University all agreed.

Indeed, Prof Anton Muscatelli said 'all power over thresholds, bands and personal allowances' of income tax should be devolved. Muscatelli once chaired an expert group for the Calman Commission whose proposals – 'ambitious and far-reaching' five years ago – are now widely seen as hopelessly outdated and timid.

In short, the post referendum period has become a very radical place.

So has the Smith Commission reflected these high hopes? In a word, no.

The Smith Commission

Robert Smith's report – dear reader, the good Lord still has a Christian name – was produced in hyper-quick time by a committee with representatives of all five Holyrood parties and published on 27 November 2014.

Despite the bold submissions, hopes weren't high that Home Rule would be delivered. After all, the Labour party only backed fiddling with income tax rates during the referendum campaign and lagged well behind the Tory and Lib Dem offers. This astonishing state of affairs doubtless contributed to the Yes campaign's triumph in Glasgow, Dundee and West Dunbartonshire and the party's projected wipe-out in these former strongholds in the 2015 General Election. In the dog days of 2014, though, the Smith Commission – created by David Cameron – swung Labour's way, devolving powers to set bands and rates of income tax but keeping the crucial power to set the income tax threshold at Westminster. It seems this compromise was produced so Labour could resist

Tory calls to exclude Scottish MPs from future English budget votes. In the end, the proposals resembled a lucky bag list more than a reasoned, logical set of choices.

It was politics by horse trading and party diktat – not a solution to reflect the will of the people.

No surprises there then.

Writing just days after its publication, it's hard to know how Scots will react. Some will note that the SNP's John Swinney and the Green's co-convenor Maggie Chapman were part of the Smith process, that the No side after all won, that some powers are better than none and that this may be a starting point not a final destination. Others, like this anonymous participant quoted by Kevin McKenna in the *Observer*, view the process more bleakly: 'Seeing all welfare powers taken away at the last minute and seeing Labour argue against the devolution of the minimum wage are things I don't think I'll ever forget. In the last hours of the Smith deliberations, the Tories were getting direct input from Westminster government departments and cutting deals with Labour to avoid anything that might affect English votes for English laws.'

How sadly predictable.

Of course, new powers were proposed including the right for Scots to run their own elections (paving the way for 16 year olds to vote in the 2016 Holyrood elections), the entrenchment of the Scottish Parliament so the Commons cannot abolish it (though it's not clear that can legally be done), devolution of Crown Estates property management (first requested in 2011) and Air Passenger Duty and an Aggregates Levy (first recommended in 2009 by the Calman Commission).

Lord Smith also recommended the Scottish Government be given unspecified borrowing powers (which must be agreed with the UK government) and the ability to top up welfare benefits like disability living allowance, the personal independence payment, winter fuel payments and the housing elements of universal credit, including the bedroom tax – if Holyrood can rustle up the extra cash. But the minimum wage, equalities legislation, health and safety, control over abortion law, most key economic levers, the Universal Credit package of benefits and the general tilt of welfare policy all remain in the hands of Westminster.

Reaction has become increasingly negative in the days following publication, despite Gordon Brown's plea to Yes supporters to hit the reset button, accept the Smith deal and move on.

On one level, the former Labour leader is of course right to suggest Scots want an end to constitutional wrangling. Folk are weary of vows, pledges, horse-trading and a greater emphasis on potential powers beyond Holyrood than workable ones within it. But there's no evidence voters blame the SNP for stubbornly stoking the fire. Au contraire. 66 per cent of Scots still want all tax and spend powers and all welfare powers located in Scotland, not just some.

Why don't they believe the Smith Commission fulfils the Vow and constitutes a Home Rule settlement?

The main reason is fairly simple – because it doesn't.

Home Rule is widely understood to mean everything but defence, foreign affairs and macroeconomic policy. Unfortunately for the unionist parties, that's a cleaner, more easily grasped idea than the assorted and hard-to-remember list delivered by Robert Smith. Some of the proposed powers are considerable, but together they are not memorable. Indeed several other pro-independence commentators hit the alarm bell not the reset button over Smith's plans to devolve income tax without compensating powers over national insurance, wealth taxes or oil and gas revenues. Iain Macwhirter described that as 'a transparent fiscal trap,' Kevin McKenna believed the deal had 'more caveats than the dowry agreement of a Tuscan princess' and Joyce McMillan called the new tax powers 'a political poisoned chalice – an invitation to Scotland's political class to increase their spending by hammering ordinary middle and lower earners, while once again letting the seriously wealthy, and large corporations, off the taxation hook.' According to Richard Murphy, a prominent English economist and tax expert, under Smith 'there is no opportunity to create economic growth, no opportunity to create redistribution, no opportunity to create the outcomes in Scottish society that any Scottish Government would reasonably want to see. What's the outcome? A mess, is the best answer.'

Matched against Gordon Brown's pre-referendum pledge of 'near-federalism' and Danny Alexander's summer-time talk of 'Home Rule', Lord Smith's compromise just doesn't cut it. Of course, all the above would be sceptical, wouldn't they? Calculations of tax likely to be controlled by Scots vary from 37 per cent of the total (Nicola Sturgeon's best guess) to 75 per cent (according to the UK government.) But even prominent No voters like the former Labour First Minister Jack McConnell hae their doots. He has challenged the government to prove that 50 per cent of taxes would be devolved. As a result, the air is thick with uncertainty about the size, scope and workability of the new powers. Leaked reports of an earlier draft suggest more powers were nearly granted. In the old days such, claims would be dismissed as SNP scare-mongering. Unfortunately for the estimable Robert Smith, a burst of last minute horse-trading along party political lines sounds entirely plausible in light of the similarly concocted Vow. Scots haven't gone through two years of soul-searching to come up with a clutch of reheated offers, a dangerously limited range of tax powers and a hard-to-entrench promise that Westminster cannot abolish Holyrood. Voters want a meaningful and memorable deal.

But British 'democracy' only ever responds to threat, gripe and agitation. Westminster elections occur only every five years – and even then hardly act as democratic validation for any particular policy or electorate. In the south east of England and in the Midlands, the 2015 General Election may hinge on immigration policy and Europe. In the north of England it may become a protest vote on continuing austerity. In Wales, parity with Scotland's proposed tax powers could be the main issue, whilst Northern Ireland could demand control over corporation tax. Little wonder that the 2015 General Election in Scotland looks set to become a de facto referendum on Home Rule. Voters understand what politicians cannot. In a deeply divided 'United Kingdom' with no fair voting system and no fair, statutory way to manage difference, each national population must sing long, hard and shrill from one hymn sheet to make any impact at all.

Evidently, too, the constitutional fire beyond Scotland is starting to catch alight. Politicians debating further devolution for Scotland have triggered demands for citizen involvement and equal treatment by parliaments in Belfast and Cardiff and by English councils. Handing extra powers to cities might look good but it would seriously disadvantage suburbia, towns and rural areas. Yet most of the English electorate appears to have little appetite for the regional devolution that would 'right-size' governance south of the border and allow symmetrical federalism across the whole UK. Clearly, the business of extracting powers from Westminster's grasp has only just begun. Why on earth should Scots – the main protagonists in that battle – lay down their constitutional cudgels prematurely?

It's also possible that Lord Smith's proposed powers may not be deliverable in a hostile Commons – or workable as the UK welfare system struggles to cope with a chaotic shift to Universal Credit and another bit of asymmetric devolution. So why should Scots ease the pressure when Home Rule – the preferred option of the majority – will soon be a central plank of SNP and Green manifestos in the General Election?

For all sorts of good reasons, it doesn't look like Gordon Brown's 'parting plea' to hit the reset button will be heeded by former Yes voters. Ironically though, that may help ensure that his dream of a 'near federal Britain' comes to pass. It's unlikely that even Super Broon can deliver federalism before he quits next May. So effectively, the battle-ready Yes camp is doing Gordon's work for him.

Aye, don't mention it by the way – nae bother Big Man.

In any case, Scotland evidently doesn't stand where she

once did – even as recently as 19 September. That's not to deny the referendum result but to argue about its overall impact. As the No-supporting impressionist Rory Bremner has recently observed, 'Scotland voted against divorce, and got engaged.' An October poll giving the SNP 52 per cent support and a projected 54 out of 59 seats in the forthcoming General Election showed where most newly engaged voters have been putting their energy. Of course the polls have swung back – somewhat. But the scale of change in the SNP's political fortunes cannot be explained away as an inevitable consolidation of the Yes vote. It simply wasn't that large. Scots generally appear to be feeling frisky and hopeful that 'one more push' – traditionally Labour's battle cry – might apply instead to the Home Rule campaign next year. The public mood in Scotland right now is to find proper constitutional solutions – not half measures.

By contrast, the political mood in London is to cut deals that keep MPs in jobs and real power at Westminster.

So all eyes are now on May 2015 and a General Election which is almost bound to see Labour lose seats north of the border, whichever of the three candidates wins the Scottish leadership contest.

It's hard to know whether Scotland's political post-referendum realignment will become permanent.

But clearly books like this will need constant updating for the next few years. And not just because of imminent constitutional change. Away from all the cross border warfare, some key sources of disempowerment identified in *Blossom* – concentrated land ownership, centralised political control and overlarge local authorities—are finally to be tackled at Holyrood.

So, to say we live in interesting times is a massive under-statement.

We live at the start of an era in which Scotland will finally blossom.

Why?

2014 was a year of education, consciousness-raising and confidence creation in which 'radical' ideas of equality became mainstream and those who voted to create an inde-pendent state realised they were well able to tackle elitism and right-size Scottish democracy instead.

So this is the new starting point for *Blossom*.

A nation – and perhaps a government – with an appetite for real social change.

CHAPTER THREE

Blossom

IDENTITY OR BAGGAGE? For several centuries – and the last two referendum years in particular – Scotland has been on a quest for one, weighed down by the other.

Some still believe that independence alone can create momentum for change. But 55 per cent of Scots opted to stay within the United Kingdom on 18 September 2014. Must we all wait for a different outcome to a second referendum before Scotland tackles long-standing problems of unfairness and inequality? Certainly independence would jump-start Scotland – just as a new home, job or even a divorce can improve a bad situation all on its own.

Sometimes though, a change of circumstance just shifts old problems to pastures new – unpacked baggage and all. Nations are no different.

Blossom – first published a year before the independence referendum – has always contended that a change of constitutional control would not be enough to transform Scotland. That was not meant to be gloomy or defeatist – it's actually a vote of confidence in the capacity of Scots to handle more power in real, reinvigorated communities than any politicians are currently offering.

Social inequality clashes with every idea Scots have about themselves – and yet it's been accepted as normal together with top-down governance, weak local democracy, disempowerment, bad health and sporting estates the size of small countries. Of course Scotland also boasts the Tartan Army, whisky exports, a social democratic consensus, Andy Murray, a wheen of best-selling authors and stunning scenery. Life is great for some and not at all bad for others so we still turn away from an inconvenient truth.

In international terms, Scotland is more often exceptional for all the wrong reasons.

We have sub-east European health outcomes, ghettoes of near unemployable people, an indoors culture and high rates of addiction and self-harming behaviour. Scotland also has the smallest number of people owning the largest amounts of land, the lowest proportion standing for election and the largest local authorities with the least genuinely local control of tax and resources in Europe. We have one of the biggest income gaps between rich and poor. And although no-one has done the research, I'd also guess we have the least outdoorsy population, the smallest number of boat owners per mile of coastline and a high number of children who aren't sure eggs come from hens.

But arguably we also have the most popular cities, varied landscape, magnificent scenery, valuable energy resources, richest inventive tradition and most diverse linguistic heritage in the UK. So is Scotland's enduring ability to punch beneath its weight caused by our enduring lack of statehood – or is it the other way around? I appreciate that's not the way most involved with the independence referendum would frame the question. I was brought up in Belfast during the 'Troubles' when even a Buddhist was asked, 'Aye, but are you a Catholic or a Prod?'

And yet whether Home Rule materialises, Westminster

parties somehow deliver 'The Vow' or Scotland holds another referendum in our lifetimes, this misunderstood, unequal, stoic and feisty wee country may be much the same for generations without internal, structural change. More constitutional powers may give the gardener a wider range of tools but fundamental problems with soil, fertility, aspect and shelter will remain unaltered. Perhaps these long-standing issues need more attention than new gadgets and levers. After all, the garden shed already contains tools that have never been used. What's been missing amongst the head gardeners has been the will and ideal opportunity to use them.

Perhaps some politicians think all in the Scottish garden is rosy relative to conditions further south. I think deep down though, Scots know there's no point celebrating when we manage to sit a point above England at the bottom of almost every international health and wellbeing league table. With our natural and human resources and our political culture, we should be setting our sights higher.

But that's hard. Even before the referendum, Scots were badly served by a political debate that's often sloganeering, simplistic and scaremongering and by a media which has become a collective echo chamber for suspicion, pessimism and despair. There is a way out for Scotland – a way for this country to truly blossom. But it needs us to question what we currently regard as normal and inevitable. And that, by definition, is very hard. Our working knowledge of the way other countries operate is limited. Likewise our real understanding of how the other half lives in Scotland itself. So we don't really believe inequality causes the shameful, premature mortality of the 'Scottish Effect'. We can't imagine the positive effect of having a wee bit of land, or a forest hut for weekend escapes. We can't conceive that a shift of investment from later life to early years could improve Scotland's social problems within a generation. We can't visualise a country where young people come first, speculators are stopped from pushing up house prices and genuine communities raise taxes and run their own services. We can't envisage how life and democracy would be improved if Scotland hit the North European average of 70 per cent turnout at local elections not nearly bottom with 38 per cent.

Most Scots simply haven't experienced life in healthier democracies where co-operation is in with the bricks, equality is a shared policy goal and entitlement is not the preserve of an elite. But nor has the average Scot sampled the other extreme – life on benefits in our own 'deserts wi windaes' – as Billy Connolly called Scotland's massive, peripheral housing estates.

So we don't know how energy-sapping that life can be. Nor do we know that some folk in these 'hopeless' communities have nonetheless created profound social change. And we don't feel the pain personally when some quietly fail – broken by a top-down system of governance which is designed and run by fellow Scots. Betwixt and between, the average Scot does not know the best of times or the worst of times. So we settle too readily for something in between. This is not to blame anyone. Social segregation means we almost all live in ghettos – quite unaware of how other people live across the great divides of class, gender, geography, occupation and sometimes religion. The referendum though has made one thing abundantly clear.

Scots have a distinctive political and social culture and are no more northern variants of the English than the Irish are western ones.

The Scottish identity is not just a bundle of remnants – a set of random behaviours by mindless contrarians welded together into a dangerously unstable and unpredictable personality. Scots are quite obviously and consistently different from their neighbours – English, Irish or Norwegian. But different enough?

Scots are (characteristically) in two minds. Some folk still believe national difference must be enormous before policy or governance arrangements need pay the blindest bit of attention. Thus Scotland must become as unlike England as Brazil is unlike Denmark before difference is worth recognising or nurturing. During the referendum campaign No supporters often maintained that Scots had the same social and political views as folk in the rest of the UK. Actually it wouldn't be surprising if that was true. Most Scots read pro-Union or London-based newspapers and watch London and Salford-based network news on the BBC. Nevertheless – and quite astonishingly given the power of conformity – Scots do hold a distinctive set of outlooks and attitudes. An Ipsos Mori poll in early 2014 found 22 per cent of folk in England regarded immigration as the Number One issue facing Britain – only 12 per cent of Scots felt the same.[1] The bedroom tax was opposed by 75 per cent of Scots but just 50 per cent of folk in south east England. Research conducted by CityUK

---

1   Bobby Duffy and Tom Frere-Smith, 'Perceptions & Reality: Public Attitudes to Immigration' (Ipsos Mori), January 2014.

consultants in February 2014 showed Scotland was the only part of the UK in favour of staying in the European Union, a finding replicated by a more recent poll in November.[2] In the 2010 Westminster elections just 1.7 per cent of Scottish MPs were Conservative compared to 20 per cent of Welsh MPs and 56 per cent of English MPs. UKIP are currently polling 19 per cent in England[3] and 5 per cent in Scotland. And of course 0 per cent of English voters have voted to leave the UK whilst 45 per cent of Scots have.

Scots are what Benedict Anderson called an Imagined Community 'because the members of even the smallest nation will never know most of their fellow-members, meet them, or even hear of them, yet in the minds of each lives the image of their communion.'[4]

You could call that a form of love – that warm, mutual feeling of confidence and trust between independent people that encourages them to join forces, share resources and change living arrangements to face the future together. But hey – love? In a debate about Scottish independence? The very idea proved far too tough for politicians in a nation that still doesn't do emotion without a large skelp of drink. So the

---

2   Scottish respondents are the most strongly in favour of staying in Europe (+18 per cent) and this is the only part of the UK surveyed where more want to stay than leave. At the opposite end of the scale, the South East (excluding London) was the most in favour of leaving Europe (-21 per cent). See 'The City Listens' (http://www. thecityuk.com/media/latest-news-from-thecityuk/the-city-listens-new-research-into-the-public-s-views-on-the-eu/), February 2014.

3   Comres poll, 27 October 2014.

4   Benedict Anderson, *Imagined Communities: Reflections on the Origins and Spread of Nationalism* (London: Verso, 1983).

official constitutional debate focused instead on detail, process, money and currency – like a divorce where hurt, betrayal and despair cannot be discussed and practicalities assume paramount and disproportionate importance.

Who will have the stereo – and can its future be sensibly discussed in isolation from the CDs? At many points the debate on both sides was arid in the extreme.

Of course, as Better Together boss Blair McDougall recently revealed, it was No campaign policy to keep a relentless focus on the economic and the practical difficulties of independence and resist any temptation to widen the debate.

But here's the thing. National self-determination is never just about technicalities; it's mainly about identity, confidence and trust. That's not to say the technical questions are trivial. Almost everything written about Scottish independence touched on the Black Gold. Would oil sustain a new Scottish state or did the 2008 banking collapse suggest Scotland couldn't rely on its own resources to stand alone? Could Alex Salmond guarantee Scots would be better off in an independent Scotland? Of course he couldn't. And not just because the Saudis are determined to keep oil prices low until the threat from shale gas disappears.

Is that inability to guarantee prosperity the real reasons 55 per cent of Scots voted No – or did some of the claims about shared use of the pound and an enduring social union just sound too good to be true? It's strange that every academic and his dog was involved in analysing voting intentions during the campaign, but no forensic study seems to have been made of the actual result.

Still, one thing remains clear. If Scots need guarantees and cast-iron certainty, this nation will forever remain a grudging and grumbling part of the UK. None of our small, independent neighbours broke away from larger states with a guarantee of better times. Far from it. When Norway announced independence from Sweden in 1905 it immediately became the second poorest nation in Europe. The tiny independent nation of Iceland which boasted the world's first parliament reluctantly returned to Norwegian control in the 13th century after tree-felling turned the island into a northern desert. Still its tiny population (smaller than Dundee) seized the chance for independence without a moment's hesitation when the Germans occupied Stepmother Denmark in 1944.

Back then, Iceland had no geothermal power, had not fought and won the Cod Wars, nor gambled and lost everything thanks to a bunch of cocky young bankers. What it did have, was a sudden influx of American soldiers at the Keflavik airbase, radiating confidence, driving jeeps and promising to stick around. And then Iceland took a leap in the dark.

So it goes. The urge to break away from an existing union – political, marital or financial – is rarely totally rational, or economically prudent. There may be preparation, debate and plans – but eventually caution becomes an anchor and the voyage must begin.

Mind you, Scotland has been approaching the constitutional question with yet another current running – localism. It may not be necessary for Scotland to prove its people are dramatically different or guaranteed to have short-term economic success or even part of an imagined community to argue that 5 not 55 million people is an ideal size for democracy and effective governance – especially with a public sector dismantling government at Westminster.

Culture, oil, politics, history and size. Scots have as many reasons as any other restless nation to consider independence, although in 2014 the No argument finally proved more persuasive – or less frightening.

Some prominent English commentators did get the point, though. English socialist Mark Perryman and *Guardian* journalists George Monbiot and Deborah Orr believed the departure of the collectivist Scots might provide a long overdue jolt to the complacent English left. Others – like ex-*Sun* editor Kelvin MacKenzie – accused the Scots of being whingeing subsidy junkies and demanded a halt to the 'gravy train' north. Mind you, I'm sure he thinks the same about Yorkshire.

If the campaign for Scottish independence had been taken seriously in England when it was launched in 2013, the whole UK could have had a long overdue debate about federalism, devolution and democratic change. It didn't happen.

It was far easier to portray Scotland's endless agonising over constitutional status as a right royal pain. We do want more powers, don't we? A bit... no a bit more... no that's too much... no maybe it's fine... What about a referendum with one question... Or two... no, wait...

It was easier to mock Caledonian indecision, view Scottish independence as Alex Salmond's personal obsession and his party's landslide majority in 2011 as a form of mass hypnosis. It was just too difficult for the metropolitan chattering classes to regard the plodding Scots as a revolutionary vanguard – the only folk really able to challenge Britain's centralised, top-down system of government.

Until – months before the vote – even the naysayers could see that something had changed. The packed town hall meetings, enthusiastic mass canvasses, grassroots movements and general explosion of creative energy on the Yes side, topped by THAT 51 per cent opinion poll persuaded even the hardened cynics that Scotland was in the grip of a truly (and enviably) special experience. The historic turnout was viewed with genuine awe by weary London hacks, until the prospect of southern UKIP by-election victories hauled their attention back south. But radical possibilities live on in the Scottish political scene. The SNP and Scottish Greens have seen their memberships treble. And tens of thousands of local Yes campaigners could mobilise again if Smith vs. Home Rule becomes the battleground for the General Election, if delivery is botched, if a UKIP/Tory coalition at Westminster looks likely, or if a sharp exit from the EU seems to be on the cards. 55 per cent of Scots opted to give the Union one more try – that's true. But general dissatisfaction with Britain's elitist way of working was made clear. And that has finally kick-started a wider debate in the rest of the UK about centralisation, the interchangeable austerity of the main UK parties and the creaking, archaic nature of British institutions.

Will that debate roar into life in England as it did in Scotland earlier this year? Probably not. Already devolution for English regions has been successfully translated by the canny Conservatives into English Votes for English Laws and more power for some Northern cities. Who will press for more?

The Welsh? Gubbed by their neighbours in 1283, our Celtic cousins were forced to dance to an English tune in education, health, local government, housing and even political outlook, despite devolution. The distinctiveness of Wales is largely cultural, not political or institutional. Welshness is kept alive by male voice choirs, Welsh language schools, s4c, the Methodist Chapel and (once upon a time) by campaigns against holiday homes. No-one can be in any doubt the Welsh are culturally distinct from the English. But has that been enough to create equally strong feelings of nationhood or a drive towards a new Welsh state? Like defiant prisoners whistling 'Home of our Fathers' as the firing squad take aim, Welsh culture has been the last defence against economic and social domination. The Scots have always had more – we've had unique, long-lasting institutions. No offence to speakers of Welsh, Gaelic or Scots, but language alone does not sustain nor fully define a nation – at least not this one.

Law abiding, rational, dour old souls that we are, Scots are defined by outlooks created by institutions that predate (and have survived) the Union. By an education system that seeks breadth, not specialism. By a legal system based on statute, not precedent. By a Kirk not led by the Head of State. By a housing policy not historically based on sale and inheritance, but (for better and worse) on tenancy and rent. By an economy based (for most of last century) on state activity not private enterprise. And by an endless and hopeless quest for kinship and connection in lieu of the social democratic state, Scots have lacked the opportunity (and single-minded determination) to build. All that most Britons notice about Scots is that we wear kilts – but who doesn't these days – and have two public holidays at Hogmanay.

In fact, we do many things differently north of the border but since we don't quite understand why ourselves, there's no reason anyone else should. As a result Scots are often propping up what doesn't matter and ignoring what does. Occasionally we catch the scent of a blossom that has been taken from the room – like Hugh MacDiarmid's little white rose of Scotland that 'smells so sweet and breaks the heart'.

The move towards a more equal, Nordic-style society has begun. But the move is hesitant; partly because radicalism is still defined by rudderless, conservative Westminster and partly because progressive Scots – divided by the recent battle for independence – will probably be divided again by the 2015 General Election.

There's no doubt Scotland has a distinct, national identity. Not all good. But not all bad either.

The task for Scots is to let that flower blossom – to dismantle shade-creating, top-down structures of governance and weed out the negativity and self-doubt caused by the persistent blight of inequality.

Scotland's new First Minister, Nicola Sturgeon, has committed herself to this very task.

And amazingly, transformation looks likely to happen first in the unchanging, private world of Scotland's large land owners.

CHAPTER FOUR

Land, land everywhere... and soon a drop for sale

SCOTLAND STILL HAS one of the most concentrated patterns of landownership in Europe – fewer than 500 people own more than half the land, rivers, lochs, mountains and forests. The first Land Reform Act of 2003, which gave communities the right to buy land when it comes up for sale, didn't make a massive change to that grim reality beyond the crofting counties of the Western Isles.[1] The Scottish Government cannot finance more than a few community land buyouts each year and individuals cannot get their hands on small, affordable parcels of land. In 2014, the ball is still in the court of the large landowner.

In 1997, the people of Eigg, working together and flat-out for eight long years, raised more money in a public appeal than the combined value of all their own homes and turned the tide of Scottish history.[2]

Eigg demonstrated that land reform is about people not

---

1 142 applications to register a community interest in land were submitted under the Land Reform Act and 95 were approved. Of these, 33 had the chance to go ahead and purchase land and 11 were successful in doing so, according to Scottish Government figures: less than a one in ten success rate. See www.outlaw.com 26 September 2012.

2 Eigg was purchased on 12 June 1997 for £1.75 million by the Isle of Eigg Heritage Trust (which took over from the Isle of Eigg

soil, the present not the past, and it is relevant to every Scottish community, not just remote ones. And yet an Eigg-style buyout is still a giant leap from a standing start for most communities. As a result, the chain of (largely Hebridean) buyouts has become an ever-growing exception to a still dominant rule of quasi-feudal land ownership. Which means stultifying 'Old Eigg'-style situations are being tolerated by people across Scotland right now, while help is focused on communities able to bid successfully for limited public cash.

Certainly the 2003 Land Reform legislation has helped communities buy land, islands, bridges, pubs, wind turbines, libraries, orchards, woodlands and farms and these ventures have been life-changing for all involved. But there isn't enough cash in Christendom to fund the purchase of every parcel of land, forest or water, nor the energy amongst unpaid volunteers with day jobs. And actually, why should there be? Community buyouts alone cannot reverse the disempowerment experienced all over Scotland today. The community on Eigg is now one of Scotland's most capable – tackling everything from depopulation and climate change to saving the corncrake. But it's been empowerment the very hard way. In more democratic countries with no history of feudalism, community buyouts are unknown. In Norway, for example, land has been owned or rented on long secure leases by tens of thousands of individual Norwegians for centuries. All rural communities also own common land – often planted

---

Trust), a partnership in which Eigg residents have the majority of trustees along with representatives from Highland Council & the Scottish Wildlife Trust.

with trees and co-operatively managed to yield a local income and steady supply of wood – and controlled through small municipal councils.

So there are no community buyouts in Norway. Widespread land ownership, land taxes and local control mean Norwegians communities don't need to buy what individuals already own and voters democratically control. The community buyout is a typically piecemeal, Scottish solution to a larger problem we haven't had the will to tackle universally, systematically or at source. Those who work hardest may escape the blight of feudal-style land ownership. Those who can't, must bide their time. Don't get me wrong. The amount of money involved in community buyouts has produced amazing returns from relatively small investments. But the wider system has remained intact – and until a few months before the Referendum vote, there seemed no prospect of a solution. Not because Scottish politicians lacked the powers – but because they lacked the will.

This inconvenient truth was often mentioned during the long independence campaign. At many meetings, undecided voters suggested the SNP's unwillingness to decentralise power or act on land reform was evidence that independence might bring little meaningful change. New boss, same as the old boss was a much repeated fear. But the radical final report of the Land Reform Review Group (LRRG) in May 2014 took cynics by surprise. After a lacklustre interim report a changed committee with a refocused brief produced a game-changing final report.

The LRRG called for an upper/maximum limit on land

holdings, the imposition of business rates on sporting estates (they currently pay nothing), a right-to-buy for agricultural tenants and an end to the distinction between inheriting land (where spouses and children have no legal rights) and 'moveable' property like houses (where they do).

The Scottish Government promised to consider the report and submit a new Land Reform Bill before the next Holyrood elections in 2016. Civil servants who might have been negotiating independence began drafting that legislation instead and in late November, an adventurous programme of land reform took centre stage in Nicola Sturgeon's legislative programme.

There is a consultation period, during which Scotland landowners will doubtless make loud protests. But if the Bill goes ahead unchanged, Scotland's big landowners must prepare for intervention in their hitherto private domains.

The Land Reform Bill will re-introduce business rates on sporting estates (they currently pay none) and use the proceeds to boost the Land Fund for community buyouts to £10 million per annum until 2020. It will introduce a new power for Ministers to intervene where the scale of ownership or conduct of landowners is a barrier to the sustainable development of local communities. That could check acquisitive new landowners like billionaire Dane Anders Povlsen whose Highland purchases have apparently made him the second biggest landowner in Scotland after the Duke of Buccleuch. It could also let Ministers intervene where communities feel existing landowners are such poor custodians of the land (and the buildings they allow tenants to lease) that local communities are unsustainable.

The Bill will also place duties on trustees of charities with large chunks of land to ensure effective engagement with local people over the way they manage it – that could tackle a recent trend of large estates being managed by a hard to access trust, whose private decisions nonetheless have huge public impacts on house-building, community development and the viability of local businesses. Companies owning land will have to be registered in the EU – not offshore tax havens.

A separate Bill on Succession law will democratise inheritance so children and spouses have equal shares of the land in their parents' estate – currently siblings only have equal title to property. It's already been claimed this could cripple small farms which might not be viable if split into three or four equal units. That's true. That's why, in most neighbouring countries with equal land inheritance since the days of Napoleon, one sibling will often 'buy out' the others to let the farm continue viably and ensure the keenest farmer takes over not just the eldest. The need to properly compensate siblings has also helped fuel the Nordic cabin culture – brothers and sisters are often given a bit of land on the farm to build a weekend hut in lieu of cash. It's true that as land values rise, it gets more difficult to 'buy out' other siblings. But the same problem applies to inherited property. Somehow, reasonable systems tend to produce reasonable solutions. And no country seems to think that favouring just one child is any kind of answer.

Essentially, the Scottish Government has initiated changes which have stood the test of time in almost every neighbouring democracy – changes that will release the natural forces of inheritance to encourage the organic break-up of large estates into more manageable, affordable, varied and accessible land parcels.

Finally, after centuries of secrecy about the extent and value of land holdings in Scotland, there is to be transparency with a Scottish Land Register that will contain detailed information on all government-owned land within five years. That may be an optimistic timescale unless more resources are committed to the task. One council land lawyer told me that she might take 50 rather than five years to complete the task – and that's dealing with wings of government that are required to comply. Without extra staff and powers of compulsion the task of gathering accurate information from reluctant private landowners may be even more difficult.

Perhaps, given the Scots' long experience of exclusion from the land, the Scottish Government could create a visible, symbolic building where a physical copy of the Land Register can be inspected by Scots and homecoming visitors to gain basic information about the land they regard as home. Finally, such an idea is at least possible.

The Bill will also create a new democratic terrain relating to land ownership, populated by explicitly interventionist institutions like the Land Reform Commission. And Nicola Sturgeon has promised to review the council tax allowing campaigners to argue for land taxation as a better replacement which could shift the burden from those on low incomes, stimulate the economy and present landowners and speculators with a financial incentive to 'divest' fallow acres and unused buildings or face eye-watering tax demands.

But that all lies ahead. So too does action to allow greater access to land and Scotland's marine heritage – many rivers are timeshared into the next century, many lochs are effectively out of bounds and the coastline and foreshore are still managed by a distant Crown Estates Commission (even when the powers of that London-based body are devolved).

The prospects for tenant farmers are less clear. Across Europe tenant farmers usually own their farmhouse and around 100 acres of surrounding farmland – they only tenant or lease extra land, to allow for flexibility. In Scotland however, tenant farmers tend to own nothing – not even their own farmhouses – no matter how large or profitable their farming operation. That means many live without security, and therefore without the opportunity to borrow against their property to buy equipment or make improvements. According to historian Professor Jim Hunter, a tenant farmer's right to buy would be the most significant measure to help break up large estates, partly because it would happen quickly, whilst the other changes might take years: 'By enabling virtually all of Ireland's tenant farmers to buy their farms and advancing cash to help them do so, the Wyndham Act of 1903, eliminated big estates from Ireland and made the entire country, both south and north of the present border, a place where farms and smallholdings are overwhelmingly owner-occupied.'

Will the same thing happen here?

The Land Reform Review Group did propose a conditional Agricultural Tenant's right to buy – but the issue was taken out of land reform legislation to be considered in a separate review chaired by Environment Secretary Richard Lochhead. Tenant farmers fear this means lawyers and landed interests will persuade the Scottish Government that championing their rights will be a bridge too far. By the time you are reading this, we should know which way the pendulum has swung.

So is the land reform package too radical – a 'Mugabe style land grab' as some critics have suggested? Any innovation in a stubbornly unchanging landscape will always seem threatening – but Scotland is only catching up with the more transparent and democratic way the rest of northern Europe has managed land for centuries. Scotland formally abolished feudalism only a decade back so the trappings of that cap-doffing culture are still firmly in place across rural Scotland. The presumption that land will always be too expensive for local use – even when derelict – also sits unexamined in many cities. The urban empire of the land speculator must be the next to fall.

If passed, the combination of recommendations in this new Land Reform Act will see large estates break up 'naturally' into more manageable, diverse blocks over time. But the onus for action will still fall upon individuals and communities – a daunting prospect in areas where the landowner has been landlord, employer and big cheese for generations. Certainly it may take years before land is more accessible for rural housing, businesses and farmers. As David Cameron of Community Land Scotland says; 'The acid test will be whether in a decade's time… Scotland's land is still largely owned by a small and privileged elite.'

Scottish politicians have had the power to make these changes since 1999, but lacked the political will, fearing perhaps that a doubtful, timorous public might not support the concerted change needed to face down landowner protests and modernise Scottish society.

Thanks to the activism and awareness-raising of the Referendum Summer of 2014, though, that fear has been largely erased. Now we are witnessing a revitalised Scottish Government which can hopefully depend on Labour and the Lib Dems in parliament and tens of thousands of well organised activists outside to support change.

In finding the courage to free up land, the Scottish Government is also freeing itself from a harmful reliance on large landowners to deliver policy objectives as varied as renewable energy targets, reforestation and rural housing.

It may take legal effort to stop some landowners circumventing new laws and physical effort to reverse decades of soil degradation and overgrazing in some areas. But there's no doubt that with democratic stewardship and new non-traditional landowners, a thousand flowers could blossom – quite literally – as the Highland monoculture of the sporting estate makes way for long-denied diversity, negligent and monopoly landowners are removed, trust-run landowners must involve communities in land-use decisions and the Crown Estates Commission finally transfers land and income to the Scottish Parliament which will in turn pass responsibilities and cash onto relevant councils.

It would have helped reboot democracy if that cash had o'erleaped councils and been handed directly to coastal communities. But that kind of change is still a way off.

Either way, there is no doubt the latest Land Reform Bill will make a long overdue start on this massive task.

How massive? Well, in his seminal book *The Poor Had No Lawyers: Who Owns Scotland (and How They Got It)*, Andy Wightman observed that 25 per cent of large estates have been held by the same family for over four centuries, and the majority of aristocratic families who owned land in 1872 still own it today.

Indeed, it's more than a century since an open challenge to Scotland's concentrated pattern of landownership was last mounted.

In 1909, Tom Johnston's exposé of the Scottish aristocracy *Our Scots Noble Families* became a controversial bestseller. He noted with outrage that just a century earlier miners and salt workers were 'bought and sold as part and parcel of the pits in which they were condemned to work for life,' and he recounted Hugh Miller's description of a 'slave village' at Niddrie Mill near Edinburgh where the collier women, 'poor, over-toiled creatures,' carried coal up a long stair inserted in one of the shafts, 'shifting a hundredweight from sea level to the top of Ben Lomond with each day's labour.'[3] The young journalist then 'exposed' the people he blamed for such exploitation – every noble family in the land:

> The Scott's of Buccleugh [sic], descended from border thieves, land pirates and freebooters, still boast their pedigree. The blood of knaves and moonlighters has by process of snobbery become blue blood; lands raped from the weak and unfortunate now support arrogance in luxury.

---

3 Brian Osborne, in his introduction to Thomas Johnston, *Our Scots Noble Families* (Argyll Publishing, 1999).

And Johnston famously concluded:

> Today in Scotland our artisans and peasants appear to
> believe that these ancient noble families hold their privi-
> leges and lands at the behest of Divine Providence; that
> their wealth has been justly earned and that their titles are
> but rewards for honest service to the state. The first step in
> reform... is to destroy those superstitions. Show the people
> that our old nobility is not noble; that its lands are stolen
> lands – stolen either by force or fraud. So long as half a
> dozen families own one half of Scotland, so long will
> countless families own none of it.

This angry revolutionary went on to become the outstanding
secretary of state for Scotland in the wartime coalition under
Churchill, who finally brought electricity to the Highlands by
compelling landowners to make land available for hydro-elec-
tric dams in support of the war effort. And yet even with such
formidable power, the exceptional Tom Johnston could not
push any further against landed power.

This is the scale of Scotland's historic land problem – a
problem that could soon be undone. We are not there yet –
legal change is not yet in the bag. Some powerful figures in
the Scottish Government may doubt that land reform is a
pivotal issue in a largely urban country. Agricultural tenants
may miss out and it may take decades before landowning
patterns in Scotland are noticeably different.

In the meantime, Scotland's law and tax systems still
encourage vast estates and absent landowners and stifled,
frustrated communities like pre-buyout Eigg exist across the
country. In such areas, questions about the way land is owned

are still regarded as rude, personal gripes or a sheer irrelevance. Yet we are physical creatures who experience the world first and foremost via the patch of earth that supports and surrounds us. To ask who owns it is simply to pose a basic question about democracy and human development. A nation has no greater asset than its people and yet the energy of many Scots has been wasted, in a mass of uneven battles for basic human rights over centuries. It took 65 people on Eigg eight years and a community buyout to simply issue each island tenant with a lease. No wonder Scots have been ground down. No wonder a grim air of defiance is all many have inherited. No wonder people have left. The miracle is that so many have stayed. Those hardy souls have self-selected as stoic beyond belief and thoroughly adapted to their environments. To lose them now would be to lose an essential building block in a delicate human ecosystem. And yet, those precious people are still leaving rural communities for the age-old reasons – no land, no housing and no prospects. The good news is that once government throws its weight behind ordinary people, they tend to do pretty well. Eigg is now thriving in its own eccentric, co-operative, creative and eco-friendly way and the buds of hope and capacity still exist in each patient, thwarted community. The job of a democracy is simply to shift heaven and earth to let those buds blossom.

And in the most successful democracies, that has meant devolving power and cash to local communities. Not in Scotland.

CHAPTER FIVE

Supersized Councils
– Disempowered Communities

ANYONE WHO THOUGHT 18 September represented the end of constitutional debate in Scotland must realise by now they were much mistaken.

It's as if Scotland's collective and long suppressed immune system has been kicked back into life by the two-year campaign, providing energy for a clear-out of broken, old structures and appetite for real social change. Attention has focused on the arm wrestling competition between Holyrood and Westminster. But there is an equally important struggle between Holyrood and councils and a never ending battle between Scotland's powerless communities and every other statutory level of government including quangos, Holyrood, Westminster and above all, Scotland's supersized councils.

The average population of a Scottish council is a whopping 163,000 people while the average population of a European council (with much the same powers) is far closer in size to Scotland's old parish councils (see Figures 1 and 2). It's true that most of our European neighbours have county councils around the 163,000 mark. But they also have a smaller, more loved, more vigorously contested and more vibrant 'delivery tier' of powerful, community-sized councils as well – usually called kommunes or municipalities.

Scotland, along with the rest of the UK, doesn't. Our 32

Figure 1: Scottish Councils in 2014 (left) and county and parish councils in 1929 (right) – closer to the EU average size of council today.

enormous councils try to do everything – the strategic co-ordination work of a county council and the truly local delivery work of a parish council. It's an impossible task and it's the community level that suffers. Genuinely local simply doesn't exist in Scotland – except where hard-pressed, determined, unfunded, voluntary groups have decided to fill the structural void and pump life back into their communities. I sense raised eyebrows.

How does this picture square with the Scotland of a hundred Highland Games, several dozen *Feisean* (Gaelic

	Average Population Size	Average Geographical Size (sq km)	Turnout at Local Election	Number of sub-national governments			Ratio of Councillors to Citizens
				Local	County	Regional	
Austria	3,560	36	73%	2,357	99	9	1 : 200
Denmark	56,590	440	69%	98	5	-	1 : 2,000
Finland	15,960	1,006	61%	336	2	-	1 : 500
France	1,770	17	64%	36,697	101	27	1 : 125
Germany	7,080	31	60%	11,553	301	16	1 : 400
Italy	7,470	37	75%	8,094	110	20	1 : 600
Spain	5,680	62	73%	8,116	52	17	1 : 700
UK	152,680	601	39%	406	28	3	1 : 2,860
Scotland	163,200	2,461	54%*	32	-	-	1 : 4,270
EU Average	5,630	49	-	-	-	-	-

Figure 2: International comparison of council size and voter turnout.[1]

learning festivals), night schools, sports clubs and folk nights? Surely Scotland is full of particular places – distinct, fiercely defended by their inhabitants and loved.

That's all true. But it's true despite the official structures – not because of them. The keen volunteers who make life vibrant and interesting don't formally run the places they light up – 'local' units of governance are too large and elections are too dominated by political parties. Towns, villages, islands and communities are all run by council headquarters in larger settlements elsewhere.

And it's been like that for a while.

---

1 Jimmy Reid Foundation, Silent Crisis Report 2012.

The democratic heart of 'small town' Scotland was ripped out in 1996, when 32 unitary authorities replaced 65 old style councils – nine regions, 53 districts and three island councils. Mind you, the big local downsizing had already occurred. In 1975, a mixter-maxter of more than 400 counties, counties of cities, large burghs and small burghs was swept away and before that, in 1930, 871 parish councils were axed as democratic structures (though they still exist for census purposes).

That's quite a change. In my own village in Fife, for example, rents paid in the village for council housing were once used to employ 'the drain man' who went round unblocking drains, gutters, roans and pipes. Now we are part of Fife council, with headquarters 40 minutes distant, there is no local 'drain man' and flooding is so common, flood alert road signs are stashed all the way along main routes into Perth – 'for convenience'. Meaningful village control largely disappeared in the 1930s. Meaningful town control went in 1975. And after 1996, many places became non-existent – in the eyes of the authorities at least.

Those reforms probably saved money and looked more efficient on paper. But they also severed the vital link between people and place in Scotland.

So this is where the 'best wee country in the world' is currently run – somewhere else.

A creeping centralisation has taken place over decades and has accelerated on the SNP's watch. Public opposition to single police and fire services seemed to take the Scottish Government by surprise during the referendum campaign. But the U-turn over armed police didn't solve the problem. It just removed the most vexatious manifestation of a larger democratic deficit. But change seems to be coming to Scotland's supersized local government arena too.

In April, the Commission on Strengthening Local Democracy set up by the Convention of Scottish Local Authorities (COSLA) boldly highlighted the hollowing out of power in grassroots Scotland which has left Scotland's councils with the smallest number of councillors, the least competitive elections, the smallest proportion of local income raised locally and the lowest election turnouts.

The Commission's interim report observed:

> Big government and big local government have struggled to address and improve the pattern of outcomes and inequalities in Scotland because these occur at a very granular, local community level. Big systems also struggle to engage with the diversity of Scotland's communities because they are conventionally geared towards uniformity and standardisation.
>
> A new ideology in Scotland would mean setting aside the idea of 'the state' (at national and local level) as a higher authority which holds and controls resources and power.
>
> It would mean accepting that strong local democracy cannot be designed from the top down and that it must be empowered from the bottom up. Letting go of our old ways of thinking may be daunting but that is the challenge we set out.[2]

---

2 http://www.localdemocracy.info/2014/08/14/time-to-rebuild-scottish-democracy-what-the-referendum-decides/#sthash.HS2mLqiD.dpuf

Such clear-sighted, straight talking about the extraordinary largeness and remoteness of Scottish democracy was long overdue – because supersized councils are about as healthy as supersized fast food meals. As the Commission's final report recognised:

> For a country with Scotland's relative wealth and strength, the level of inequality today is simply intolerable, and has huge social and financial costs. There is a link between the absence of strong local democracy at the moment and the prevalence of inequalities.

> It is communities that empower governments at all levels, not governments that empower people.

Amen to that.

And yet, the COSLA report didn't set the political heather alight.

No wonder. Scots were immersed in the final months of the all-consuming referendum campaign. And the disconnect from all things local is so profound most Scots (including political activists) have no idea how atypical Scotland's local government system has become.

Put bluntly, it is weird.

To take just one example, the average size of Scotland's vast councils (163,000) would result in just two councils for the whole of Iceland. In fact – even after recent mergers – Iceland has 74 councils.

The average council in Germany has around 7,000 inhabitants and occupies 15 square kilometres. The average Scottish council has 20 times more citizens and covers a massive 990 square kilometres.

Swedes earning less than £35,000 per annum pay no taxes to central government, get their energy from companies run (not for profit) by local councils and put their names down enthusiastically for high-quality, council-run old folks' homes.

France, Germany, Spain, Sweden, Switzerland, Norway, the Netherlands and Belgium all have much smaller, municipal councils with higher local election turnouts, more folk standing for election (particularly women and young people since councils are closer to home), more tax-raising clout and fewer disempowering, top-down governance structures.

If Scotland was governed like the rest of Europe we would have several hundred councils – not just 32. Towns like St Andrews, Dalkeith, Helensburgh and Methil would run themselves. Islands like Barra, Skye and Mull, likewise. As it is, the Scottish Government only plans to devolve extra powers to island authorities which had the nous and nerve to pipe up during the referendum campaign. But why does Lewis deserve more power than Islay or Cumbernauld for that matter?

Across Europe, local means the size of a small town – not a small country.

Until recently this 'inconvenient truth' was simply noted by local government leaders defending their own fiefdoms against micro-management by Holyrood. But now COSLA has placed the need to devolve power beyond existing councils centre stage – and to put it crudely, when turkeys start discussing Christmas, you know something important is happening.

COSLA President David O'Neill has echoed the Christie Commission mantra – 'you cannot "do" health to people or communities – you must work with them. If the argument is that devolution doesn't stop at Holyrood, then it doesn't stop at existing local councils either.'

So far this laudable realisation has prompted a lot of talk (and the inevitable slew of pilot projects) but hasn't made a lot of difference on the ground. How could it when 'co-production' means a herd of elephants must work with a family of mice to plan the future?

What is happening, however, is a clash of professional titans as the two biggest local budget holders – health and social care – are forced to work together, pool resources, and plan jointly in Health and Social Care partnerships. In principle this is a very good idea. Duplication in service delivery means 17 services were involved in the care of one unemployed mother – to quote a much publicised case. Delayed discharge from hospitals is stressful for patients and massively expensive for taxpayers – but it still happens because the centrally funded NHS has relatively expensive beds but the locally funded social care department hasn't got small amounts of cash for relatively cheap home support and adaptations. Clearly – shared budgets can end this nonsense tomorrow as long as territorialism, defensiveness and proceduralism can be overcome. Can they?

There is an incentive for councils to play ball. According to COSLA Chief Executive Rory Mair a single, central National Care Agency may take responsibility away from councils altogether if they prove incapable of joint working. But where in all of this is the incentive to involve, empower or even 'sub-contract' delivery to communities?

If nothing less than constitutional entrenchment and

protected funding is good enough for Holyrood in its dealings with Westminster and local government in its dealings
with Holyrood – how come un-funded and un-elected groups
at community level are still perfectly OK?

Community Councils in Scotland have an average annual
budget of £400 which has to be spent on stationery. They have
no statutory functions, no need for election if few candidates
stand and only 'advise' councils on minor issues. Admittedly
Highland Council has given its community councils slightly
bigger budgets and in West Perthshire five community councils
have grouped together to exercise more clout with the mighty
Perth and Kinross Council. But in 2013, members of Grange-
mouth Community Council quit en masse when government
ministers gave the go ahead for a combined heat and power
plant they had opposed for the previous three years.

Whatever the rights and wrongs of that individual case,
one thing is clear. Community councils in Scotland only have
influence when local authorities allow it. Just to rub salt into
the wounds, English town and parish councils fare better
with an average budget of £750,000 funded by a precept on
council rates. But that tier of community control in England
was recently judged the least powerful in Europe – which
means the tiny nano-democracy of Scottish communities is
effectively non-existent.

In the absence of beefy community councils, local Development Trusts manage local assets like libraries, housing and
wind farms – some have multi-million pound turnovers, others
are picking up functions, premises and services off-loaded by
cash-strapped councils. But Trusts are not elected by the whole

community – good because party politics rarely get in the way of action but also bad because they can't claim to democratically represent 'the community' on every issue.

According to the Scottish Government the forthcoming Community Empowerment and Renewal Bill will let communities and development trusts take over underused public sector buildings and assets. But councils and quangos will still be able to drag their heels, confound volunteers and charge full market rates for sales and leases. In some places community empowerment will happen. In others it will simply offer the chance for burnt out volunteers to engage in yet more unequal struggles with the legal departments of oversized councils and remote quangos so that libraries, old folks' homes, leisure centres and other important social functions can be saved from impending cuts.

That's not good enough.

What Scotland needs is a formal system of small, delivery sized councils with budget, statutory powers, perhaps taxraising powers and mandatory elections.

Instead what Scotland gets are more well-meaning chances to meet and dream.

In November 2014, for example, 400 folk gathered amidst torrential downpours for Scotland's first Rural Parliament in Oban. The event eloquently reflected the nature of power in rural Scotland. The venue was not a council facility but a community owned and run sports centre. The group was addressed by speakers from rural parliaments in Sweden and Estonia. Estonia has a population of 1.1 million people and 193 councils. Swedish kommunes are effectively Home Rule.

By contrast, Scotland's new rural parliamentarians went home to communities that lack any formal power to change anything.

The Community Empowerment Bill doesn't tackle this power vacuum – it neither turns community councils into dynamic new delivery level authorities nor does it knock them on the head and put them out of their misery.

'Local' in Scotland currently means a strategic, regional level of governance no other nation in Europe would regard as 'community sized' – none that is except the rest of over-centralised, top-down Britain.

Thanks to this void at the local level, Scotland's experience of community-led social enterprises has also been weak. Unlike Ireland, we have failed to embrace credit unions. Unlike the Nordics and Spaniards we have failed to establish cooperatives. And unlike any nation intent on dismantling oversized, disempowering bureaucracies we have failed to protect Scotland's only real 'self-help' success – the community-controlled housing movement in Glasgow. But times are changing.

Internet crowd-funding has introduced ordinary people with cash to ordinary people with marketable ideas. The result has been successfully crowd-funded films, books, online magazines and housing projects. Community shares have also established investment vehicles like Garmony Hydro on Mull. Some people still believe it's up to the financier, council leader, lottery official or government funder to kick-start change. But others have decided they've waited too long for these authorities to deliver and are taking matters into their own hands.

Ironically, many of these impatient community activists are also members of the Yes campaign – how long will they tolerate a Westminster-style deaf ear about the need for real devolution of power to communities by their own Scottish Government?

CHAPTER SIX

Women – The Real Indyref Winners

FROM THE VANTAGE point of December 2014, Scotland looks set for a *Borgen*[1] kind of future.

One Scottish Labour leadership candidate, the Scottish Conservative leader and the Green co-convenor are all female. And of course Alex Salmond's successor as leader of the SNP, Nicola Sturgeon, is Scotland's first female First Minister.

With a female 'look' to politics, a northerly latitude, a population size of five million and (until 2007) experience of coalition governments – Scotland might seem familiar to Denmark's fictional *Statsminister*. But there the resemblance ends.

Compare how the two nations spend money and on what. Compare who decides and at which level of government. Compare how highly equality is actually rated, how much voters trust politicians and how much politicians trust local communities to run themselves and deliver services. The conclusion is inescapable. Scotland is top-down, elitist and unequal. To use Geert Hofstede's classification of nations, Scotland is masculine to its bootstraps.[2]

---

1 *Borgen* is the unexpectedly popular political drama shown on BBC4 about Denmark's first female Prime Minister and her impact on Danish society.

2 Geert Hofstede wrote a seminal book called *Cultures and*

You could make many relevant comparisons between Denmark and Scotland – here are two.

Firstly, childcare costs in Scotland are amongst the highest in the OECD – whilst Denmark's are amongst the lowest.[3] A sobering new report by Citizens Advice Scotland shows 25 hours a week childcare for under-twos in Scotland accounts for 27 per cent of average household income, but just 12 per cent across most of the developed world.

Provision here is patchy – only a quarter of Scotland's local authorities think there is enough local childcare, 25 hours doesn't cover the hours of a full-time job anyway, school holidays pose an extra headache and provision is worst for shift workers, those on zero-hour contracts, country dwellers and disabled children.

Not surprisingly then, fewer women in Scotland work – 65 per cent in 2010 compared with 74.4 per cent in Denmark where high quality full time childcare costs a maximum of just £300 per month. In large part, that's because the British welfare model supports families via behaviour-modifying tax

---

Organisations in 1980. From 1967 to 1973, while working at IBM as a psychologist, Hofstede collected and analysed data from over 100,000 employees in 72 countries. From those results and later work, he developed a model for comparing cultures. One comparison talks of 'masculine' countries which encourage elites to pull everyone up by competing for resources and 'feminine' countries which try to improve average performance through cooperation. On that register, Sweden is the world's most feminine country – the UK is number 62.

3   Rob Gowans, 'Working at the Edge: Childcare' (Citizens' Advice Scotland), December 2014.

credits (favoured by Gordon Brown) which means parents must pay first and reclaim (some) costs later – whilst Danes put cash straight into childcare subsidies with much greater social and economic effect.

Our Nordic neighbours think differently about investment in human capital.

They sometimes have shabby community centres, unpainted doctor's surgeries and ice-splintered roads – but they never neglect basic investment in people and children the way we do.

In Norway, every child has a statutory right to a kindergarten place from the age of one until they are six or seven with a maximum means-tested parental contribution of £200 per month. Norwegian children spend the bulk of the day outdoors – often in snow and sub-zero temperatures – fully equipped in snazzy, thermal, waterproof gear. Some kindergartens are even co-located with farms so the kids can feed and play with animals. I visited the Medas nursery near Bodo where children collect eggs, grow tomatoes, make hay and even watch slaughtered cows being dissected to learn more about animal biology. The Norwegian belief is that children divorced from the cycle of life and death become estranged from nature and are less independent, confident, co-operative and happy as young adults. An activity centre in Arctic Bodo is part of every local pupil's week – especially children with autism, learning difficulties, hyperactivity or truant tendencies. They drive on quad bikes, abseil on cliffs, climb trees, drive go-karts and eat and learn outside around sheltered camp fires – even in winter. As educational pioneer Henny Aune puts it, 'children have more physical energy than adults and children with attention issues have more energy still. They just need to run it off. Then they can focus'.

Is such a humane, outdoorsy and practical approach to life possible in Scotland?

I can hear the objections already. Too expensive. Alright for the Nordics. A luxurious irrelevance when essential school services are being cut. Destruction of the 'mother-at-home' parenting model which has worked for generations. Of course, some traditional societies do score highly in the UNICEF child wellbeing index. In Cyprus, for example, there still are families with four children, two grannies, two parents working from the home and sundry relatives and cousins around. The chances are high that toddlers in this environment will get the engaged play which is vital for development. But here's the big news. Very few Scottish families these days have four kids. Or two parents who stay or work at home. In fact, the average family unit consists of two working parents and 1.4 children – so it's hard for each bairn to be constantly engaged. Some parents have substance abuse problems – and that makes sustained play during those vital Early Years well-nigh impossible.

That's why smart modern, industrial societies provide excellent, affordable childcare. Not because big, traditional families don't do a good job of child-rearing, but because we don't live that way anymore and evidence suggests the earlier children socialise in a stable environment, the sooner they start to thrive. The Nordic approach is not only humane and sensible – it gets better results. The sort young adults need and employers actually want.

Scottish employers placed the following skills top in a Future Skills survey: planning and organisation, customer handling, problem solving, team working and oral communication. When are these missing 'soft' skills learned? Between birth and three years old. Which age-group still gets least education spending in Scotland? Birth to three. And which age-group gives the maximum 'bang for educational bucks' according to Nobel prize-winning economist James Heckman? Three year-olds. How are soft skills most easily acquired at the age of three? Through engaged play in traditional, extended families or in highly social kindergarten. And what are we doing?

Keeping kids in splendid isolation at home or sending a few to under-funded nurseries until the school gates swing open and working mothers can finally get affordable day care for their children at primary school. Is four (in Scotland) or six/seven (in the Nordic nations) the best age for children to begin school? We can't even begin to have that discussion.

So Scotland will keep spending millions trying to retrofit skills onto the teenage and adult casualties of substandard childhoods in the belief that happy, healthy kids are a luxury we cannot immediately afford.

Of course it's true that our Nordic neighbours are independent countries, able to fund big changes of policy by rebalancing entire budgets. But central government in the Nordic nations doesn't have supreme control over purse strings or local, political priorities. It does have the social power to bestow rights upon children and the economic clout to provide subsidies. But it's the people in relatively tiny local councils who have decided to transform the life chances of women and children by spending their taxes on the best childcare in the world.

By contrast, in Scotland, we have a remedial society – which spends relatively little cash on the formative early years, stores up social difficulty as neglected children become unemployable adults, and then makes harsh judgements upon those who fail.

This unchanging, grimly predictable pattern of public spending means most single parents will continue to live in poverty and their children will go on paying the price – no matter how well stoic mums and dads shield the adults of tomorrow from the stresses of today. These are the downsides of a masculine society. No matter how many times a few prominent women speak, the priorities of successive Scottish governments speak silent volumes. Scotland urgently needs a wider economic strategy to put lost value back into the domestic sphere. We won't get that until economists recognise the household as a source of value and creator of wealth and we won't get that as long as male economists dominate the political sphere. 'The purpose of studying economics is… to learn how to avoid being deceived by economists' said British post-Keynesian economist, Joan Robinson.

She was right. If the home was recognised as a source of value in the economic system, as the late feminist economist Professor Ailsa Mackay argued so persuasively, the Scottish Government could more easily justify plugging 'leakages' which lower productivity through absenteeism and under-performance.

A British think-tank, the Resolution Foundation, has calculated that the crippling cost of childcare means a million women are 'missing' from the UK workforce. Pro rata, that's a whopping hundred thousand women missing in Scotland – a problem for our economy, for parents (often single mothers living in poverty) and for their children.

But despite all this evidence backing the vital importance of good childcare, Nicola Sturgeon's modest proposal to extend free childcare to all three and four year olds and vulnerable twos has been described by some as a threat to the traditional family and an unaffordable burden on Scottish taxpayers. Ochone.

In a world dominated by the narrow values of business 'giants' like bickering tycoons Donald Trump and Alan Sugar, it doubtless sounds naïve to suggest better childcare will improve the wellbeing of tomorrow's citizens and the employment chances of today's mums. But since women have been working outside the home in almost equal numbers to men for decades, the household has been losing labour and energy and that loss must be stemmed. One answer is the availability of universal, state-subsidised childcare as the building block of free education for all. And yet, when capital investment is under discussion, childcare is rarely mentioned. That should matter more to economists than childcare activists. It still doesn't.

Gender quotas and shovel-ready Scotland

The new First Minister is clearly determined to win the necessary 'permission' from Westminster to introduce gender quotas on public boards, since the hoped-for devolution of equality powers was not recommended by Lord Smith.

But if winning the argument about childcare in Scotland is tough, getting the public behind 40 per cent quotas for women could prove even tougher. Firstly, gender quotas are not already standard in councils or parties like the SNP where it might have been easier to start than public boards and quangos. Opponents roll out the argument that women don't want to be token appointments. Strangely though, few blokes worry about the near certainty of having been token men during their careers – chosen only because of their male gender. Still, the prospect of being promoted beyond their capabilities is enough to make some women wary of 'special treatment'. Not myself. I've 'progressed' in life to become the outspoken and largely unemployable person I am today, as a result of several acts of positive discrimination when I was younger. Without them I would have waited patiently for a turn that never came like so many other women.

Ironically though, women's quotas in Scotland have mainly been deployed by the SNP's rivals. Scottish Labour twinned seats by winnability and the SSP, Greens and Lib Dems all 'zipped' candidates on party lists in the first 1999 Holyrood elections.

Now Nicola Sturgeon is boldly advocating quotas for the

public domain without any history of such mechanisms being used in her own party. That's brave. It's also what leadership is all about. But the task would have been easier if quotas were already common – not just to get public opinion on board but to help produce a range of empowered lasses ready to take up the new opportunities on offer.

A second problem is that many capable women don't feel remotely attracted by the apparently elitist world of the boardroom. Decisions taken in health boards and quangos may have massive impacts on Scottish lives. But capable women throw far more energy into the voluntary sector and social enterprise. Is that because the public domain appears too hostile, high pressure and exposed? Or is it because Scotland lacks training grounds for higher public office? These exist in countries like Norway where union membership is still high and councils are 12 times smaller than Scottish councils. That means one in 81 Norwegians (many of them women) stands for election compared to just one in 2071 in Scotland.

In many ways, Scotland is following a Norwegian template, but cannot easily recreate the supportive conditions that allowed Norway's male, Conservative trade (not equality) minister to astonish everyone in 2003 by proposing a 40 per cent quota of women board members for the largest companies on the Oslo Stock Exchange.

At that point, Norway already had 40 years' experience of women's quotas on public boards, local councils and quangos. But now the largest, most profitable firms in the private sector were targeted and the tough penalty for failure to comply caused uproar. Disobedient PLC's would simply be shut down. Not surprisingly, companies toed the line. Over a decade the proportion of women on the boards of the 300 largest Norwegian firms has risen from 7 per cent to 42 per cent.

According to research, men on these boards now behave more professionally while women turn up more often, come better briefed and tend to be more in tune with customers. Since female board members are more risk averse, they can also check the more excessive behaviour of men caught up in testoster-one-charged 'groupthink.' Eight countries, including France, the Netherlands and Germany, have followed Norway's lead and the European Parliament is about to request that all member states do the same – although the UK looks set to opt out.

Of course, there are problems. 13 per cent of Norwegian PLCs became limited companies to avoid the quota laws. Some women do hold several board positions – but 'quota queens' are almost matched in number by 'quota kings'. According to Bergen academic Arne Selvik, 'The mere presence of women in closed groups is disruptive and that improves productivity.'

Businesswoman Mai Lill Ibsen thinks women should learn to invest, seize economic power and try to find a partner with an open mind about breadwinning. Her own banker husband raised eyebrows when he took three months off after the birth of their first child. 'By child number two that was expected.'

It has taken Norwegians with ultra-local councils, active trade unions and a system based on cooperation and trust half a century to make quotas work. Must Scots wait so long? According to Arne Selvik, 'Maybe contagion will prove to be contagious. With Nicola Sturgeon, Scottish women have a role model and a great opportunity for swift social change.'

So perhaps the Nordic moral is that progress does become self-reinforcing – as long as it begins. And the First Minister probably has the power to make sure that happens at public board level, whether that has the overwhelming backing of the public or not.

The second big difference between Scotland and Denmark is the attitude of each country towards welfare. Danes see welfare as a way of redistributing income across the lifetime of each individual (making deposits during working years, and withdrawals during child-rearing, illness, retraining and old age) as well as redistributing income between people. So the Danes provide high-quality services for all to keep welfare attractive for the affluent and affordable for everyone else. That increases social solidarity, and that keeps the rich paying taxes with relatively few complaints. Clearly, that virtuous circle has been broken in Britain – Scotland included – where anyone with enough private cash is expected to opt out of poor-quality state provision and finance their own pension, healthcare, kids' education and parental care.

Even though Social Democrats have lost their monopoly on power in each Nordic state – and even though free schools and private providers are more common – no new Nordic governing party has dismantled the basic model. There is no political 'ping pong' or pendulum swinging with the election of a new government every five years. There is general political and social consensus. Danish Professor Jon Kvist has put it succinctly: 'Without high levels of female employment there's not enough tax income to fund the Danish welfairytale.'

The social investment policies of the Nordic countries not

only mitigate social ills but also prevent deep social cleavages.

Despite the advances promised by Nicola Sturgeon – doubling free childcare for toddlers – Scotland, hand on heart, cannot say the same. Yet.

So as things stand, Holyrood could no more replicate the backdrop to *Borgen* than BBC Scotland could produce it. Danish State TV's surprise international hit revolved around real, believable, independent-minded women – because Danish life does the same. Literally. A year after *Borgen* was first broadcast in Denmark, the young, engaging mother of two and leader of the Social Democrats, Helle Thorning-Schmidt, actually did become the country's first female prime minister.

The strongest Nordic fictional characters – Birgitte Nyborg and the fearless, damaged heroine of the *Millennium Trilogy*, Lisbeth Salander – were created by Adam Price and the late Stieg Larsson. New Nordic men have created strong, believable female fictional characters which have become international feminist icons. That's only possible when fiction mirrors reality.

Of course neither Denmark nor Sweden is nirvana. Even in a world where powerful, capable men take responsibility for childcare, share power and occasionally play second fiddle, things go wrong. Egos appear. Marital stress remains. Promises aren't kept. Good intentions aren't realised. And women in positions of power occasionally act nasty and find they still can't have it all. That perhaps is the real fascination of *Borgen* for politicians like the new First Minister. It doesn't create female characters as sidekicks, victims or female versions of

Alan Sugar. It suggests women are perfectly capable leaders but observes no-one can be perfect and there is often a high personal price to pay for professional success. All of which is patently true.

But one thing's for sure in any country. Without conscious change and active intervention by government, presumption, entitlement and exclusion keeps gender segregation eye-wateringly extreme. Scotland is living proof.

Scottish Enterprise figures show women constituted 0.9 per cent of Modern Apprenticeships in construction and 97.8 per cent in childcare in 2008, making up just 22 per cent of the total. This is perhaps the most polarised take-up of apprenticeships in Northern Europe and means the number of Scottish women able to gain employment in construction, building or engineering projects is practically zilch. That matters, because Scottish politicians and civil servants have backed construction projects as the best way to kick-start the economy, restore optimism and provide jobs. And so it would be – if women worked with shovels. Female employment is the perfect strategic tool for a Government that wants to increase equality and stimulate demand, women have been hit hardest by job cuts and service reductions and more of a woman's wage is spent immediately (and especially on children). Unfortunately though, very few Scotswomen are involved in construction. Yet in 2013, Scotland's Finance Secretary, John Swinney, published a list of preferred 'shovel-ready' projects including £34 million worth of trunk road schemes, a £5.7 million revamp of ferry ports, £308 million for NHS buildings and £65 million on college upgrades. Of course, building projects are important and of course the SNP were trying to appease powerful sectors in Scottish business before 2014. But what about the powerful sector called women? 2013 could just as easily have been the Year of the Soft Hat – with £394 million invested in human capital, not road junctions. And it's just possible that might have made some women think differently about their prospects in an independent Scotland.

The independence gender gap

Ironically, since women voters were more dubious about the merits of Scottish independence than men, women's issues got a higher profile during the referendum campaign. And despite the No vote, that clout has not diminished.

News of a sizeable indyref gender gap hit the headlines with a Panelbase survey in March 2013 which found men were almost twice as likely to support independence as women (47 per cent against 25 per cent) and observed the 22 per cent gender gap was actually growing (it was 15 per cent in 2012, according to Ipsos Mori).

Small wonder then that Alex Salmond used his leader's address at the 2013 SNP Spring conference to reach out to women voters, saying a 'transformational shift towards childcare should be one of the first tasks of an independent Scotland'. That single prominent plug meant childcare finally made it onto newspaper front pages – for a whole day. But the pledge was highly conditional – it relied upon independence so taxes from women returning to work would boost the childcare-subsidising Scottish Treasury, not Whitehall. The pledge also contained very little detail and therefore prompted a stack of questions.

Could Nordic-style public services be delivered without also raising taxes to Scandinavian levels? Perhaps not. Of course the Scottish Government could ask middle-class parents for some cash – in Norway there's a maximum contribution of £200 per month for each full-time, high-quality kindergarten place. It could – but it won't. Since the 'something for nothing' speech by Johann Lamont, the SNP has been determined to provide free public services without the merest whiff of personal contribution to put clear blue water between itself and Scottish Labour.

Alternatively a new Scottish welfare system could try to cover the childcare subsidy by scrapping British tax transfers and switching cash directly to services instead (à la Denmark). But the Smith Commission hasn't recommended such sweeping powers over welfare and the next independence referendum is probably some way off.

Still, the No vote hasn't shut down the possibility of an Early Years revolution for one simple reason.

The Scottish Government simply cannot fail Scottish parents and progressive voters.

For one thing, women are now a well organised force in Scottish politics – particularly on the Yes side. The first large post referendum Women for Independence meeting in Perth attracted 1,000 women, the next in Glasgow sold out a 500-seat venue in a single weekend. In the space of just one week, two months after the vote, I spoke at a Radical Book

Fair event in Edinburgh, a branch meeting of the SNP in Erskine and a gathering of Highland Green activists in Farr. All were full to overflowing with Yes-leaning Scots and probably more than half the audience were women – of all ages. Something has changed in Scottish society. Women used to be the least active or politically organised part of society – not any more.

So the cavalry is coming to help some children – in 2016. If the SNP begins to deliver transformational childcare and greater social equality, it could 'seal the deal' with once-sceptical women voters. The party can also use childcare to argue that only Home Rule – not the weaker Smith Commission proposals – can expand the Scottish economy to finance further change. There is simply no way not to deliver the childcare pledge. And no way a fudged half-measure will work either.

Social reforms that are too timid and conservative waste time and please no-one. Weak AV voting reform looked so fatally flawed that PR supporters campaigned against it. Likewise the limp Scottish Assembly proposed in 1979 and John Prescott's toothless North-East assembly in 2004. The Scotland Act is still being 'improved' by unionist supporters even though that slow-moving charabanc has been overtaken by the referendum and now the Smith Commission – itself likely to become history as soon as a new Westminster government takes over. That's what happens when politicians heed the noisy, entitled and important… and miss the boat of popular opinion.

Thanks to the extraordinary levels of political engagement and self-education achieved during the referendum, most Scots know a child-friendly, people-friendly society is a difficult but possible destination – if spending priorities change and economic levers are cleverly and confidently deployed in pursuit of progressive policy goals not the maximisation of profit.

The evidence is all around. That well-known revolutionary feminist organ *The Economist,* for example, compiled its own 'glass ceiling index' in 2013 to show which countries give women the best chance of equal treatment at work. Based on OECD data for 26 developed countries it compared the number of men and women in tertiary education; female labour-force participation; the male-female wage gap; the proportion of women in senior jobs; and net childcare costs relative to the average wage. The top ten (in order) were New Zealand, Norway, Sweden, Canada, Australia,

Spain, Finland, Portugal, Poland and Denmark. The UK came 18th – after Israel.

Six of the top ten have populations of ten million or less and all but one is a 'feminine' society by Hofstede's classification. That's a strong argument for the SNP as it tries to win women voters. But there's a catch. Small countries do better for women – but only when they've jettisoned the 'winner takes all' masculinity that characterises the UK and present-day Scotland.

Can that happen? Has the desperate need to woo women voters during the indyref created an opportunity for long-term social change – even a feminist agenda – in dear old Macho Caledonia? Perhaps it has. And perhaps that's the way social change often happens.

Swedish women had to be opportunistic in the 1990s when they extracted better childcare, maternity and paternity rights and candidate quotas from reluctant political parties after threatening to establish a Women's Party. Norwegian women got subsidised kindergarten as the price of their re-entry to the paid workforce after acute labour shortages in a country with no colonial immigrants to fall back on.

Are Scottish women ready to flex their collective political muscle?

Or despite the gigantic meetings, are women doomed to remain frozen out of the formal political process? Strathclyde University's John Curtice wrote in 2013:

> Perhaps in inviting us to step boldly into a bright, but as yet unfamiliar future, the rhetoric of the Yes camp is one that resonates more with the hunter-gatherer, assertive side of our natures rather than our desire for calm and security. And stereotypical though the observation might be, maybe this appeals to fewer women than to their male, more macho counterparts.

And yet, David McCrone's research has shown women were just as likely as men to 'feel Scottish' during the referendum campaign and be even more interested in health, education and inequality.[4] If women didn't associate these key issues with the constitutional debate, perhaps that says more about the way the debate was conducted than female fear of change. Hesitation about independence could even be seen as a

---

4 David McCrone, *Understanding Scotland: The Sociology of a Nation* (London: Routledge, 2001 2nd ed.).

rational response to the long term shortcomings of politics in Scotland – full of warm words that rarely get translated into action, great frameworks that are rarely matched by competent delivery, and the prospect of dramatic upheavals just to acquire a new boss same as the old boss – male, stale and pale.

Women don't buy rhetoric – they want concrete evidence that change (with all its disruption) will benefit all lives not just some lives. Or they tune out.

I'd guess the SNP's relentlessly cheery picture of life after independence didn't ring true for many women and that set all sorts of alarm bells ringing – easily amplified by the extraordinary constellation of forces gathered during the last week of campaigning to predict Armageddon if Scots voted Yes.

According to YouGov older voters were also less keen on independence – only 34 per cent of over 65s voted Yes compared to 55 per cent of 25-39 year olds. Why was that? Well, older folk were less likely to use social media for alternative perspectives, more likely to rely on the BBC and No-supporting newspapers and very rattled by alarmist claims that pensions would be worthless, food would be more expensive and jobs for children and grandchildren would become scarce as big business relocated over the border. But there's another factor. Most of these sceptical or frightened older voters were also female.

Women were always less likely to be won over by appeals to national pride, freedom or other 'emotional' concepts. They had to be convinced by rational arguments about practical consequences. In a debate full of rhetoric and technical preoccupations with currency, armed forces, and the nature and speed of EU membership, the everyday practical focus was easily edged out.

Despite Nicola Sturgeon's high profile and very positive public rating: +17 compared to David Cameron (-40), Alistair Darling (+1) and even Alex Salmond (+7) – every key appointment, event or policy launched by the SNP or Yes campaign left women and their primary concerns as an afterthought, or forced 51 per cent of the population into special pleading for a small share of the action. Perhaps the last Scottish Government under Alex Salmond had become a tad smug about female representation at Holyrood. The first Scottish Parliament was once the second most gender equal in the world and that environment allowed capable women to shine. When Labour stopped twinning, the gender mix at Holyrood slipped back. Today, our parliament is only number 25 in the world equality league.

Will Nicola Sturgeon now embrace quotas to tackle that in her own party?

Even the socially conservative Irish are grasping the thistle. Currently there are just 25 women TDs in the Dail – at 15 per cent of the total that's a record high. But change is coming. 30 per cent of candidates in all parties must be female in the 2016 general election, rising to 40 per cent by 2019, or political funding will be withheld.

So it looks as if Holyrood will soon lag behind the Dail – just as the SNP already lags 20 per cent behind Labour in the number of women it gets elected as MSPs.

The Irish Deliberative Assembly, which has been examining its constitution, has a hundred members – 66 citizens and 33 politicians: 60 men and 40 women.

The Icelandic Assembly was composed of 475 men and 475 women. It suggested a Commission elected by popular vote to draft a People's Constitution and the 15 men and ten women chosen in a nationwide online vote devised this opening line: 'We the people of Iceland wish to create a just society with equal opportunities for everyone.' Amen.

Across the world confident societies have used process and structure to devise more thoughtful, gender equal, adventurous and people-based constitutional processes than anything being suggested for Scotland.

It's not too late to take advantage of the independence debate and legislate now to put women at the heart of Scottish public life – for the next Holyrood elections and beyond.

CHAPTER SEVEN

What's Next – The 2015 General Election

CONSTITUTIONAL POLITICS will continue to dominate our lives in 2015 with the forthcoming General Election. It's possible that a large bloc of Yes-supporting MPs could extract full Home Rule and a decision not to renew Trident in exchange for supporting a minority Labour government. If that isn't forthcoming, the Election could prove productive for Yes supporters in a different way – if the winners don't swiftly concede full federal-style powers for Holyrood, they could trigger another referendum.

Of course, it's equally possible that the electoral arithmetic stacks up differently and the Westminster show rumbles on without providing Home Rule concessions or sufficient animus for Indyref2.

And it's possible that weary Scots will just settle for the Smith Commission proposals and revert to old voting patterns and political loyalties. Not very likely, but possible.

That's why it's important to remember something amidst all the flurry about candidates and strategies, target seats and campaigning.

Transformational change, like charity, begins at home. So the Scottish Government must be encouraged to change the top-down, disempowering, centralist agenda of many centuries to facilitate social and political change.

And there are activists aplenty to make sure that happens

– if they can turn from the bright lights and drama of Westminster to focus also on the relatively mundane world of home-grown policy change.

The signs are promising.

After most ballots, the relatively small cadre of party workers go home, voters move on and interest in the minutiae of politics quickly subsides. There is no sign that such 'business as usual' will resume in Scotland anytime soon.

Political meetings have been transformed from small cabals of time-served loyalists to massive rallies attended by well-informed people who expect politics to mean engagement not lofty speechifying from a self-appointed political class. Parties, especially the SNP, must respond to this democratic revolution or risk looking like parents who've smugly mastered PlayStation while their kids have moved onto Minecraft (google it).

A mere three per cent of Scots are paid-up party members despite the massive influx. But beyond the parties, knowledge of governance and taxation systems is at an all-time high, there is an insatiable appetite for education and difficult detail and an air of mobilisation, readiness and anticipation. Scots are like motorists who once called on the AA for every breakdown but are now determined to change tyres and fix problems themselves. It's heady stuff.

But how long will it last? I'd guess heightened public interest and a capacity to intervene decisively in the political process will become permanent features of Scottish public life as activists realise they can improve Scottish democracy by refusing to be assimilated.

That's not just a legacy of 18 September – it's something bigger.

Something that drove thousands of non-nationalists to campaign for independence in the first place. Something that connects most members of the 45 per cent and 55 per cent camps. Something that may still drive two thirds of Scots to demand full control over taxes and welfare in Scotland.

It's a deep-seated desire to modernise and democratise Scottish society in ways considered beyond the pale by the 'Mother of Parliaments' but entirely normal in the rest of Northern Europe. And that desire has grown stronger as a result of the referendum.

Look at it this way. 45 per cent of voters were quite prepared to set up an independent nation despite predictions that jobs would go, headquarters would move south, the pound would become a foreign currency, food prices would rise and pensions would be worthless. At least a further 15 per cent gave the idea serious consideration. Are such threat-hardened citizens likely to be deterred from backing a robust Land Reform Act because it looks contentious? Are they likely to be satisfied with a Community Empowerment Bill that leaves Scotland with the least effective tier of local govern-ance in Europe because it's a bit late to amend it? Are they likely to view a 38 per cent voter turnout in council elections as acceptable – or allow the promised childcare revolution to be put on hold? I doubt it. Political clout may now be more important than party membership because none of these challenges sound as formidable now as they once did.

Scots have been invigorated by this big, robust referendum debate.

The rest of the UK has not. The Yes campaign had a good thorough workout. The No parties did not.

Of course, the Labour leadership battle will try to gloss over recent splits.

But what was said in the wake of Johann Lamont's resignation will not easily be forgotten in former Labour heartlands that voted Yes and in which – according to a sensational Ipsos Mori poll – only 17 per cent now plan to vote Labour at the 2015 General Election. And though the advent of a new leader is bound to stabilise Scottish Labour, its fortunes are unlikely to change without real answers to tough questions.

Why did Johann Lamont put up with bullying from Westminster for so long? Is it part and parcel of the job – the curse of being the Scottish face of an English-based party? Why vote Labour in 2015 or 2016 if candidates are basically muzzled poodles not independent-minded, outspoken Scots?

I witnessed a horrible grilling during the summer on BBC Two's *Daily Politics* when Andrew Neil effectively told Johann Lamont she was a total political failure. The former leader sat quietly absorbing the punishment. I almost moved to intervene – the mauling was so one-sided and personally unpleasant. Now it's clear why Johann couldn't respond.

She was following orders. But how much disrespect and stress is one person expected to take in the name of political leadership? The most extraordinary aspect of Johann Lamont's resignation interview was not its salacious detail but the fact any detail was aired in public. That has never been the Labour way. Since New Labour first silenced dissenters to appear electable, dirty washing has been washed in private.

No more. Jack McConnell, Andy Kerr, Henry McLeish

and Malcolm Chisholm let rip and sounded more open, animated and alive than they've done in years. Of course, most have nothing to lose career-wise, should have piped up far earlier and may simply be legacy-building.

But it didn't sound that way. Messrs Kerr and McConnell in particular sounded like men who have decided they no longer wish to deny the existence of a distinctive political culture in Scotland and will battle openly and confidently with their Westminster 'betters' to defend it.

In that respect, Labour's present dilemma is a mirror of Scotland's enduring dilemma.

That's why a clash of political cultures still seems inevitable to me despite the No result. Scots are trying to build a more progressive democracy while folk south of the border largely back parties which blame Europe, immigrants, human rights legislation and the unemployed for Britain's decline. We are heading in different directions and one day that will come to a head. But meantime Scots must use their newly discovered political mojo to start using the powers we've already got.

This is the challenge for the new Scotland.

This burgeoning of local activism doesn't just pose questions about legitimacy for party politicians – it also questions the credentials of 'civic society'. The groups who demanded wider involvement in the Smith Commission used to have the field to themselves. Now it's clear they generally represent the formal, institutional, structured side of public life – not its vibrant, informal, unsalaried grassroots. Many folks had the same misgivings about the Scottish Constitutional Convention – it was accorded respect as a representative cross-section of

Scottish society but actually super-served the interests of the 'great and good'.

If democracy is to mean more after the referendum, the SNP cannot mimic Old Labour Party thinking – with its controlling, dominant, 'winner takes all' attitude to power and its tendency to marginalise those regarded as 'off message' or not 'our people.'

Looking forwards to the 2015 general election, the SNP could have guaranteed a different political environment by considering something genuinely radical. Something that would build on Scotland's reputation for refreshing the parts British democracy cannot reach.

Something that would, yet again, put a big idea not an arm wrestling competition at the heart of Scottish political life. The SNP could have opted to stand in the 2015 Westminster elections as part of a wider Yes or Home Rule Alliance.

But speeches at the SNP's November conference ended that prospect.

A rule change means non-party members can be selected as candidates 'to stand under the SNP banner.' But many non-members don't want to stand under an SNP banner or risk splitting the Yes/Home Rule vote by standing as a Green or independent. I certainly found myself in that position.

So the change in SNP policy will certainly allow local parties to choose new members and different types of candidate. But it hasn't quite suspended the self-interest of business as usual or created the feeling of 'specialness' and joint purpose that infused the Yes campaign.

A single, combined slate would have produced more Home Rule supporting MPs than the sum of individual party efforts and offered Scottish voters a way to enliven Westminster, obtain maximum powers for Holyrood and create a diverse, effective, left-of-centre Scottish grouping to parlay with a minority Labour government.

Now it looks as if the SNP will be the only game in town for those who want more powers for the Scottish Parliament than the Smith Commission compromise.

Maybe that's realistic. It's certainly easier. But will it make 2015 feel as special as the 2014 Yes campaign? And if it doesn't will thousands of non-aligned activists devote as much time to getting SNP candidates elected?

Of course it isn't easy to bend the rules of politics. Norway had a century of Home Rule, four decades of full independence, 30 years of proportional voting and the experience of war, resistance and occupation before its four parties could make the powerful, symbolic gesture of standing on the same shared manifesto in 1945 – kick-starting a new era of cooperation for the country.

But the power of the moment and the huge leap in democratic capability still demands something bigger from the SNP just as it demanded more from the Smith Commission, the unionist parties and the BBC.

Nicola Sturgeon has already conceded that the people will decide if and when there's to be a referendum re-run. Perhaps that same powerful, wider constituency will seek to make other important decisions.

It's entirely possible.

The creation of an independent state may not be imminent… but massive structural change is still possible.

Home Rule, Land Reform and Community Control now sit before us – a shiny parcel of change that might have seemed revolutionary at any time except the referendum's stunned aftermath.

Scotland's Year of Living Dangerously has offered more release from constraint and convention than any year since most of us were children. If Scots can refocus attention from that unattainable shiny red apple atop the tree to the windfall that lies at our feet, it needn't be over either.

And that's what has changed.

Anything is now entirely possible.

A radical and unexpected shift in Scots has taken place – perhaps as significant as the Big Vote itself. Bystanders have become organisers, followers have become leaders, politics has become creative, women have become assertive, men have learned to facilitate not dominate and independent action and self-reliance have helped create a fully tradable currency – a 'can-do' approach shared by almost everyone active in Scotland today.

Two years on, Scotland's biggest problems haven't changed. But we have.

CONCLUSION

What Scotland Needs
to Blossom

IDENTITY OR BAGGAGE? Scotland is still on a quest for one,
weighed down by the other.

It's high time we opened the heavy holdall to see what
we've been lugging around. Put simply, it is disempowerment
and mutual mistrust.

Centuries of exclusion, insecurity, exploitation, and
betrayal – largely at the hands of our ain folk. There have
been glorious exceptions. There has been formidable resistance. There has always been huge potential and inexhausti-
ble, cussed hope. And generally life today for the majority of
Scots isn't bad. It just isn't as long, healthy, productive, repro-
ductive, literate, wealthy, sustainable or creative as it could
be – compared to like-sized neighbours and the vast wealth
of our natural assets.

That either bothers you, or it doesn't.

If it doesn't, congratulations for getting this far.

If it does, welcome to the growing band of Scots who feel
stuck.

And not just stuck within a stagnant UK. But stuck with
the dead weight of mutual doubt.

Scotland can't move forward with this amount of baggage,
but we can't let go either – because the unreformed, top-down
structure of society reinforces our passivity and deep-seated
fears every waking day.

Deep down, despite the referendum boost to our confidence, we still fear Scots are somehow destined to be ill not healthy, couch potatoes not athletes, emigrants not pioneers and followers not leaders.

Centuries of inequality are taking their toll. And we know it. Some Scots talk a good game but we've played second fiddle for too long to believe the propaganda. After all, we live in the shadow of giants.

Our own mothers and fathers, grandmothers and grandfathers who endured conditions we can hardly imagine – heroes who still tower over this generation. If they could put up with their lives, what are we whimpering about? If their efforts failed to dislodge unfairness and inequality, what makes us think we'll succeed? And if their answer was to emigrate, what makes us think we can face down the odds and turn the ship around?

So some dream about the next referendum and pray it'll come round soon.

We examine policies that work elsewhere in the sure and certain knowledge they will somehow not fit in here. Our malaise is too deep.

Our self-destruct mechanism too strong. Our own goals too spectacular.

Our leaders conceit of themselves too loftily distant from our own.

Our poor, too poor. Our courage wanting. Our fondness for Big Men too entrenched. Our fear of Big Men too engrained. Some of these fears are well-founded, but most are grandiosity – the self-importance of a nation that cannot face the fact it has big but fairly ordinary problems of inequality to solve. And yet because profound pessimism is rarely verbalised (sober), our negative self-talk goes unchecked and unchallenged – growing quietly in equal and opposite measure to the unverifiable claims of progress made by governments.

We're perversely proud of it. Wha's like us?

We need change. Yet despite the referendum campaign, we fear the grave-sounding, censorious-looking, finger-wagging policy wonks and fundamentalists. They don't sound like us. They suggest change could be easy and straightforward but we still suspect it isn't. Otherwise why are things as they are? In the great intergenerational game of pass the parcel that is life, can it really be up to this generation to peel the final wrapper from what's 'ae been'? Can so much really happen on our watch?

Are we up for it? Or will we keep our heads down and prevaricate? Even though new ways of organising developed during the referendum campaign, it's not clear if that new broom will sweep the stale rooms of policy formation clean. Past form is not encouraging.

Scotland has become something of a pilot paradise specialising in one-offs, unworkable compromises, empty consultations, sticking plaster solutions, rubber-stamping and risk-averse policy – or rather policy which prefers the certainty of stagnation to the risk of success.

We also do a pretty impressive line in exclusion, blame, judgement, personal abuse and media sensationalism. All conspire to nip progressive, adventurous possibilities in the bud and make sure our democracy defines progress in the weakest possible terms – rushing excitedly to the scene of accidents instead of isolating their recurrent source. So here we are: stuck.

Stuck with quasi-feudal land ownership because politicians fear a backlash if they apply even moderate land taxes. Stuck with the worst childcare in Northern Europe because politicians won't switch budgets to children from the current generation of vocal adults. Stuck with educated women who can't join the workforce because of sky-high childcare costs. Stuck with unemployable boys thanks to chaotic early home environments. Stuck with rising bills for elderly care because service providers won't hand cash to communities. Stuck with 38 per cent turnouts at council elections because Europe's largest authorities mean 'local' is a hopelessly distant thing. Stuck with sky-high energy bills in the 'Saudi Arabia of renewable energy' because the land beneath the turbines belongs to lairds and the seabed belongs to those nice pinstriped gents at the Crown Estates Commission. Stuck with kids who don't know eggs come from hens. Stuck with density destroying low-rise city housing because no-one will champion tenements. Stuck with obesity and diabetes because politicians don't see the link between cooped up Scots and an inaccessible world. Stuck with the shortest life expectancies in Europe because of self-harming addictions, grief and powerlessness. Stuck in a 'stand there till we fix you' society because professionals don't trust Scots to heal themselves. Stuck with three times the jail population of neighbouring states despite similar crime rates because we have criminalised nuisance behaviour, because of record levels of drink and drug abuse, (despite pioneering moves on minimum alcohol pricing) and because of the hopelessness that arises from all of the above.

For jobsworths, mediating this stuckness is a worthwhile goal.

For most Scottish citizens, anything less than a jointly agreed plan for change is just a colossal waste of time.

Of course in any unmanaged garden it always looks simpler to scythe away at the wilderness, spray some weed killer and plant easy to manage window boxes. Working to change the soil structure, eliminate persistent weeds, provide shelter and support climbers and native species all takes more time, creates more work, disrupts flowering for a season or two and costs more in the short term. Anyone with the smallest patch of garden will know which approach really works. But

Scots are out of touch with nature – the green stuff outside the door and the human stuff inside our communities, families and inside ourselves.

So in general, short-term fixes suffice for problems large and small.

Mutual mistrust in Scotland has caused politicians to settle for sticking-plaster solutions partly because taxation levers are not in the hands of the Scottish Government but also because there is a profound fear of change amongst professionals.

Trust has allowed Nordic politicians (and people) to be so much bolder. Not just trust in government, but trust by the people in one another and in their shared capacity to run society from the bottom up – with minimal central interference.

Norwegians read local papers, supported by central government, made from wood pulp produced by Finnish neighbours in the world's largest mutually owned forestry co-operatives. In Norway, it is illegal to make profit from education, in all the Nordics children attend affordable kindergarten (often outdoors) from the ages of one to six and in Finland the world's highest levels of school performance are largely attributable to the qualification level of teachers – even primary school teachers have Masters degrees and the profession itself chose to loup that high barrier.

But as David Cameron surveys this rich mix of shared, decentralised power, high taxes, high standards for public services and relatively little 'opting out' by the wealthy – all the UK government wants to (partly) copy is the 'free school.' Even there the English version differs from the Swedish reality – their free schools are a recent departure from 100 per cent state provision of education and are wholly state-funded, not 'private' or allowed to select pupils by the ability to pay.

Nordic society is a different world – and a successful one, as their top places in every international league table of productivity, wellbeing, health and GDP tend to demonstrate. Of course there are scandals and upsets. But few on the cata-strophic scale of Britain, whose long-run demise began when we decided to steal and then trade goods from colonised countries instead of continuing to create value ourselves.

Without empires, the Nordics have had to develop other models. They have had to learn the value of co-operation and trust, while we burned off that essential commodity in the loads-a-money era just as we flared off gas from oil rigs.

So while we have had 'us versus them', a rampant market in every area of life and a disempowering, centralised state as the only bulwark against cut-throat competition, the Nordics have been able to resist the hollow temptation to Get Rich Quick and have performed rather better.

Of course it's helped to have the Nordic tradition of powerful, quasi-sovereign local government. It's helped to have had roughly a century of the horse-trading and compromise that comes with proportional representation, not the polarising, winner-takes-all mood swings of first past the post. It helps to have 'flat' management styles, one of the lowest income gaps between management and shop floor workers, a 'social contract' between employers and workers and high levels of workplace involvement. All these civic building blocks have helped the Nordics generate the highest levels of trust in the world and public transport systems which actually work. Copenhageners have calculated that a ten per cent increase in cycling means a saving of nine million euros in healthcare costs. That's impressive. Here we pledge to have 15 per cent of all journeys by bicycle in 2020 (Edinburgh was at four per cent in 2012) and do little more than hand out a few free helmets to get there.

People are not stupid. They know Scottish roads are too dodgy to be made safe by wearing a cycle helmet. And the emphasis on tackling cyclists not road layouts or motorist behaviour tells would-be cyclists everything they need to know. Cars rule. The more helmets are handed out and the more onus for safety is placed on individuals, the less parents want their children to be out cycling at all.

More advanced societies know safety is built, not worn. I use this protracted cycling analogy only to demonstrate the dynamics of 'stuckness' across Scottish society. We are constantly producing 'cycle helmet' style temporary solutions to problems that require structural change. We should have been building up the stores of mutual trust and grass-roots capacity to pull a whole society free from the centrifugal force of what's ae been. But we haven't. So Scots struggle to really believe that rational people, with equal opportunities, early years support and local control will do reasonable and even impressive things with power where possible. Scots have long had a stronger conception of 'society' than our southern neighbours. But without the mutual trust and shared practice of democracy which are the building blocks of society, we're not 'living the dream'. Scotland has been running on empty for decades.

We urgently need to top up. Instead Scottish politicians demonstrate their lack of faith in ordinary Scots with every centralising act, failure to empower, bottled decision, bound-to-fail compromise and displaced debate about something trivial.

Might independence have changed this stuckness? Perhaps.

Taking control over all economic levers, making a statement to ourselves and to the world, taking responsibility and doing things 'our way' would doubtless improve things faster than staying in the increasingly regressive UK. But how much faster and what is 'doing things our way'?

Whatever the Great and Good have decreed?

Whatever isn't the way they do things south of the Border?

Whatever doesn't alarm the rich, powerful and landowning

classes in whose interests one of the world's most unequal societies has slowly evolved?

It's not enough to say choices in an independent Scotland would be made by the Scottish people. Of course they would. But such a response abdicates the responsibility that comes with leadership.

Our politicians are self-evidently not practising 'home rule' or genuine democracy in the bit of the pitch we already control. To progress further each Scot must first have a touch of the ball – we must all move forward together. That cannot happen while political elites dominate, men speak for women, the middle classes speak for everyone, the central belt speaks for small town and rural Scotland, vested interests thrive, power is centralised, communities are left to sink or swim by their own voluntary efforts and the disabling virus of life-shortening poverty rips through some lives and every conscience.

Devolved Scotland is not promoting 'home rule' and independent-mindedness where it matters most and has been absent longest. In ourselves. In our communities. In the places where 90 per cent of our life choices are made. On home turf.

Not every problem in Scotland is explained away by London mismanagement.

We experienced unfairness and appalling inequality long before the Union. We are tolerating inequality now despite substantial devolved power. Until our political leaders tackle, pinpoint, or start to name the destructive dynamics at work in Scottish society, we will all be stuck with them. I realise the timing of the referendum was not exactly crafted. Doubtless the SNP wanted longer to demonstrate their competence. That's my point completely.

Instead they should have been demonstrating OUR competence.

Scots need no more well-meaning proxies, smarter bureaucrats or distant saviours. If I'm not trusted to help run the place I call home, if it's better for the land to be owned by one absent Duke, if it's more efficient for local decisions to be taken on my behalf by one distant stranger, if it's fine to decide the future of my community over its head like an unconscious patient, dissected by volume house builders and privatised utilities, if it's okay for me to know my children will never, ever be able to afford homes near me, if the land I see from my window is endlessly derelict or hopelessly unaffordable, if my experience of being a parent is guilt-ridden and stressful because support to work will never, ever be affordable – if all of these realities are brushed under the carpet, then to be honest I will hardly care whether Supreme Power lies in Edinburgh, London, Brussels, Angela Merkel's kitchen, Beijing or Timbuktu.

I exaggerate for effect. Somewhat. This is not to argue against a future Yes vote. It is to say independence without empowerment is a recipe for no great change. It is to say there are other debates in Scotland as important as independence and their exclusion hasn't simplified the case for constitutional change – it has weakened it.

Certainly, Nordic nations like Iceland and Norway had longer periods of nation-building with substantial devolution before they 'took the plunge.'

The huge involvement in civic life by all Norwegians made the final leap towards independence much easier. If nature and nurture shape the young – then the hand that rocks the cradle is vitally important. As with children, so with nations.

The SNP can only be midwives of Scottish independence, not mothers.

No matter how much they want to deliver a new nation, it must be conceived, shaped, brought to life and nurtured by Scots. And not just the coalition of the willing that was the Yes campaign – but all Scots.

So the tough question is – are we in shape?

Have the political classes been building the public's democratic muscle, have we been extending ourselves, improving our democratic diet, sharing the load and spreading responsibility? The answer in most areas of political life is only maybe.

The shameful 38 per cent turnout at local elections in 2011 was a sign that the vital signs of Scottish democracy are perilously weak.

That's why ordinary Scots need more involvement in democratic life, given the scale of heaving lifting ahead – not less.

It's why we urgently need to become unstuck through unexpected breakthroughs, new perspectives, social progress – now not later.

Empowerment of all Scots is the only solution to the Scottish Effect, the Scottish Cringe, the Sick Man of Europe, No Mean City and the Empty Glen – and all these phenomena are as important to resolve as the constitutional question.

More revving the engine, more effort and more breast-beating by the influential few cannot compensate for the continuing failure to involve or empower the by-standing majority. Community effort in buyouts, community-led housing, voluntary effort in charities and self-help approaches to health show what's possible when Scots take the initiative.

But the noxious fumes from this relentless machine of top-down, paternalistic governance minimise the spread of local achievement.

Heeding siren voices with persuasive models from more unequal societies than our own (like the United States) is no use. We do not need to get any better at temporary fixes. We need to get better at creating permanent, systemic solutions. So we need to learn from societies that operate without copious amounts of Band Aid or binder-twine.

That's not to say a new Scotland will be a carbon copy of Norway, Denmark or any other state. It's not possible, or desirable. In fact, better possibilities await a nation that comes late to the business of peaceful transformation – greater relative improvements can arise as soon as we acknowledge the downsides of our disempowering legacies.

Ordinary Scots have traditionally owned, run and controlled less than ordinary folk in other neighbouring nations. Scots have therefore benefitted less from economic improvement and (shorn of the chance to invest in land, river, loch, house or even village hall ownership) we have had only one way to spend rising incomes since the war.

We have consumed it – whether on food, drink, cars, bling or the superficial, false-status conferring symbols of a nation whose people have little access to things of lasting value.

The Norwegians, by contrast, invest their cash in weekend huts, skis, ski-mobiles, excellent public transport and affordable heating.

They invested their wealth because they owned their natural assets.

We ate our wealth because we didn't.

It could still be otherwise. It must be.

We can turn and look at that stubborn bit of barbed wire on which we have become stuck. We could recognise lack of progress isn't our fault or really any individual's fault – it's the inevitable outcome of a political system. We have rushed towards constitutional change while inequality holds us back.

It's time to turn and study the problem because it isn't insurmountable. We must believe nurture not nature turns people sour – and start to nurture better straight away. After that – with the substantial powers of a new Home Rule Parliament – we can expect our own hardy wee blossoms to thrive like any others.

Scotland is currently snagged on the past, not the monster of our own nature – but fear of losing momentum stops us looking round.

And yet a cool, calm survey of the situation offers only hope. Official indifference may have created hostility towards authority – but adversity has also created connectedness, community and a voluntary skillset second to none. This unacknowledged capacity and these under-valued skills could make a seismic transformation to Scotland if they were at the heart of our democracy, not fighting constantly for credibility, funding and recognition – by right not occasional hand-out.

Despite having it beaten out of our parents, the Scots and Gaelic languages are still on our tongues and in our minds. With no official help and decades of obstruction, Allan Macrae and the Assynt crofters led the way and the people of Eigg transformed their little corners of the Hebrides to become internationally recognised models of rural regeneration.

Despite their lack of academic credentials, Ron Greer and Derek Pretswell proved no part of Scotland needs to be written off as a barren desert or an empty glen. Glasgow has become the community-owned housing capital of the UK and dozens of tenant-run groups are ready to undertake whole community-making in the style of Phil Welsh and West Whitlawburn. Tommy Riley proved the poorest, sickest men in Drumchapel could heal themselves. The internationally acclaimed obstetrician Mary Hepburn has showed how poverty can (and cannot) be shifted.

And the Scottish Referendum Campaign has proved that Scots can mobilise.

But the clock is ticking. Tommy Riley, Phil Welsh, Charles McKean, Ailsa Mackay and Allan Macrae all died during the writing of *Blossom* – prematurely and much missed. Like the little white rose of Scotland, they survived hard times and official neglect. Who would not be there when the clutter and debris of centuries is finally cleared and that hardy plant can finally blossom?

If this wee book has whetted your appetite,
I hope you'll delve into the pages of the full
Blossom: What Scotland Needs to Flourish.

Blossom: What Scotland Needs to Flourish

Lesley Riddoch
ISBN: 978-1-910021-70-5 PBK
£11.99

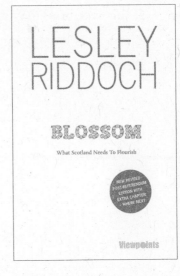

Since the referendum, bystanders have become organisers, followers have become leaders, politics has become creative, women have become assertive, men have learned to facilitate not dominate. Independent action and self-reliance have helped create a 'can-do' approach shared by almost everyone active in Scotland today. Scotland's biggest problems haven't changed. But we have.

Weeding out vital components of Scottish identity from decades of political and social tangle is no mean task, but it's one journalist Lesley Riddoch has undertaken. Dispensing with the tired, yo-yoing jousts over fiscal commissions, Devo Something and EU in-or-out, *Blossom* pinpoints both the buds of growth and the blight that's holding Scotland back. Drawing from its people and history as well as the experience of the Nordic countries, and the author's own passionate and outspoken perspective, this is a plain-speaking but incisive call to restore equality and control to local communities and let Scotland flourish.

A brilliant, moving, well written, informative, important and valuable piece of work.
ELAINE C SMITH

Not so much an intervention in the independence debate as a heartfelt manifesto for a better democracy.
ESTHER BREITENBACH, Scotsman

Luath Press Limited

committed to publishing well written books worth reading

LUATH PRESS takes its name from Robert Burns, whose little collie Luath (*Gael.*, swift or nimble) tripped up Jean Armour at a wedding and gave him the chance to speak to the woman who was to be his wife and the abiding love of his life. Burns called one of 'The Twa Dogs' Luath after Cuchullin's hunting dog in Ossian's *Fingal*. Luath Press was established in 1981 in the heart of Burns country, and now resides a few steps up the road from Burns' first lodgings on Edinburgh's Royal Mile.

Luath offers you distinctive writing with a hint of unexpected pleasures.

Most bookshops in the UK, the US, Canada, Australia, New Zealand and parts of Europe either carry our books in stock or can order them for you. To order direct from us, please send a £sterling cheque, postal order, international money order or your credit card details (number, address of cardholder and expiry date) to us at the address below. Please add post and packing as follows: UK – £1.00 per delivery address; overseas surface mail – £2.50 per delivery address; overseas airmail – £3.50 for the first book to each delivery address, plus £1.00 for each additional book by airmail to the same address. If your order is a gift, we will happily enclose your card or message at no extra charge.

Luath Press Limited

543/2 Castlehill
The Royal Mile
Edinburgh EH1 2ND
Scotland

Telephone: 0131 225 4326 (24 hours)
email: sales@luath.co.uk
Website: www.luath.co.uk

LESLEY RIDDOCH is an award-winning broadcaster, writer and journalist. She writes weekly columns for *The Scotsman*, *The National* and *Sunday Post* and is a regular contributor to *The Guardian*, BBC *Question Time*, *Scotland Tonight* and *Any Questions*. She is founder and Director of Nordic Horizons, a policy group that brings Nordic experts to the Scottish Parliament and produces a popular weekly podcast. Lesley presented *You and Yours* on BBC Radio 4, *The Midnight Hour* on BBC2 and *The People's Parliament* and *Powerhouse* on Channel 4. She founded the Scottish feminist magazine *Harpies and Quines*, won two Sony awards for her daily Radio Scotland show and edited *The Scotswoman* – a 1995 edition of *The Scotsman* written and edited by its female staff. She lives in Fife and is married to an Englishman who grew up in Canada.

Reading Lesley Riddoch's Blossom *is like inhaling fjord air after being trapped in a sweaty backroom. Just brilliant.*
PAT KANE, singer and columnist

Inspiring, galvanising analysis of the untapped potential of Scottish people power.
KARINE POLWART, singer/songwriter

Blossom *confirms Lesley Riddoch's reputation as one of our top campaigning journalists.*
PAUL HUTCHEON, The Herald

Luath Press is an independently owned and managed book publishing company based in Scotland and is not aligned to any political party or grouping. Viewpoints is an occasional series exploring issues of current and future relevance.

Cracking. A hopeful antidote to so much empty nastiness in politics. Read!
ALYN SMITH MEP

It's brilliant – every politician in the land should be made to read the chapter on inequality. I love the human stories in the book, but it's rich with evidence too. The most engaging social policy book I've read in ages (ever?).
JENNY KEMP, Zero Tolerance Campaign

I'm reading Blossom *right now and every paragraph crystallises the nebulous sensations of deep divide inequality and snobbery I have experienced my whole life.*
DES DILLON, writer

Blossom *is something we should all be reading. This is the book William Power and Edwin Muir should have written … a fine work.*
ELSPETH KING, Director, Stirling Smith Art Gallery and Museum

To all progressives – just to everyone… read Lesley Riddoch's Blossom. *She just gets it.*
DAVID GREIG, playwright

Blossom *reveals a Scotland full of promise, whose richest resource – her people – remains untapped. Riddoch's belief in Scotland's countrymen and women is the lifeblood of* Blossom.
NEWSNET SCOTLAND

A hard-hitting tour-de-force and a characteristically feisty contribution to (and beyond) the present constitutional debate.
PADDY BORT, Product Magazine